T0272805

Introduction

My first book for Green Candy Press, *Cannabis Regeneration: A Multiple Harvest Method for Greater Yields* (2015), was aimed at establishing regeneration (that is, the ability to grow and then regrow the same plant over and over) as a viable alternative to the traditional methods of growing from seed, or through the process of cloning. I proposed that all three techniques—seed, clone or regeneration—were equally useful, and attempted to prove it.

With follow-up articles in *Marijuana Venture*, *Weed World* and *High Times Magazine*, the word spread. It's great to see the procedure being discussed and used. The technique has even been included in the third edition of Greg Green's *The Cannabis Grow Bible*—a lovely acknowledgment.

We are the bud seekers. We look through the monthly cannabis magazines, eagerly searching out the quality specimens. Same with seed catalogs and lush advertising spreads. Whether we are looking for a specific strain of cannabis to grow or just a great baggie for recreational or medicinal purposes, we all want the same thing—the best buds, always. And why not? Since when was mediocre an option?

To pursue anything other than the best is to shortchange oneself. I contend that we can all grow and enjoy stunning, top-quality buds like the ones in this book. I also propose that it's relatively easy to do, and that it may be achieved cost-effectively;

no greenhouses, expensive lighting rigs or messy watering systems required. Basic grow principles combined with some clever techniques will allow you to grow amazing plants in very small places with little effort. Relax and grow. Your plants will always show greater potential if grown joyfully, with enthusiasm and love.

The approach to achieving excellence is something I first discussed in the regeneration book: the "ceiling of potential."

This "ceiling" is the maximum return a plant can give you if grown under ideal conditions—and it's not just yield. We're talking potency, flavor, aroma and everything we love about our plants. The potential to improve all facets is readily available.

For a moment, think back to the photographs in those glossy magazines—the stunning plants, some the size of small cars— these are examples of the potential that all great seeds carry, including the seeds that you or I may decide to grow. Pause

and think about that for a moment; it's a wonderful thought. If these huge plants are examples of the results of a good seed, then is there any excuse for not reaping a healthy harvest from a small, potted grow?

Each element of the cannabis plant's grow cycle (seed, vegetation, flowering and budding) can be tweaked with a clever trick or technique. Each of these methods will give your plant that extra chance to reach towards the ceiling of potential, one step closer to achieving Cannabliss. The more finesse used, the greater the potential for excellence. The effects are cumulative.

The purpose of this book

is to enhance the existing skills and knowledge of the beginner to intermediate grower. The tricks and tips within these pages are of practical use to anyone interested in growing truly magical cannabis, on a small scale, for personal use. This is the framework that will define the explanations outlined within. However, any of the techniques can be expanded upon (up-scaled) to any grow situation.

For the sake of completeness (and to form the foundation upon which we can bolt the fresh techniques), I will briefly cover the key elements of a healthy grow. We cannot, after all, dance on the ceiling unless the pillars supporting it are sound. I will quickly address these issues and balance them against the fresh wave of environmental concerns. Our understanding of topics such as water quality, electricity, how we use (and misuse) plastics, the cost-effectiveness of lights and so on have all changed dramatically in recent times, and how we grow must change accordingly.

Let's begin with a brief look at the home of the magic; the history behind the potential we seek. This superiority is not, by any means, something that appears from thin air, nor is it a fluke. It is hereditary.

CHAPTER 1

The Home of Potentional

Do you have fond memories of a particular time—probably long ago—when a certain strain impressed you like none before? When it blew you away, totally gob-smacked you—an experience so profound it's now lodged firmly in your memory? Yeah, that was *the* dope, man. I'd wager that you'll even remember the strain's name—and even where you smoked it.

Maybe it was Panama Red or Acapulco Gold. It could have been Congolese Red, Black African or Durban Poison. What about a Hawaiian beauty, grown in the volcanic soil surrounding Mauna Loa? You'll undoubtedly relate to something like these fine strains when you reference your own personal "best damned smoke I ever had."

The event may also have been *transcendental*. In other words, it allowed you to bring back fresh knowledge (or insight) from the "high" side to the "straight" side. I love it when this happens, and many enthusiasts can nail the exact year and strain relating to these profound experiences. Famed astronomer Carl Sagan credited cannabis with allowing him to hear and comprehend multipart harmonies within complex musical passages. He, too, brought the newly acquired talent back to regular daily life, enjoying music with a newfound insight.

My own profound experience was with the amazing Thai Sticks of the 1970s and '80s. This transcendental herb, tied onto bamboo sticks with hemp thread, did it for me. It broadened my understanding of the world, the universe, basically everything. It was the first time in my life that I could fully get my head around Einstein's equation, $E=mc^2$. To this day I crave that particular sativa. It was life changing.

Herb that facilitates transcendence, like in these examples, is—I contend—truly magical marijuana that has reached an unexpected level of potential. What is it that makes these satisfying strains of herb so special? Surely, it can't just be an occasional or exceptional growing technique. The secret, in fact, resides in the very backbone of the species—within its genetics.

Why Genetics Are So Important

The subject of genetics often appears overwhelming and hard to comprehend, a little beyond a fun and casual read. I mean to briefly discuss it here because the story is fascinating, and is directly linked to what we are attempting to achieve when we grow for ourselves. A little knowledge grounds us in the deep and fascinating history of the cannabis plant.

Dried and cured buds of the highest quality. Memories of the transcendental experience!

There is no technical jargon or math here (apart from a couple of words). Talk of alleles, filial generations, Mendelian dynamics and such complexities are best left to books dealing with the breeding of cannabis. You can find recommended titles in the Further Reading section at the end of this book.

Our discussion will not be so much about the cogs and codes that propel genetics. Rather, I'd like to address

Indica leaves tend to be much broader allowing for maximized light gathering.

the all-important genetic code in relation to the personal, small-time grower. This is the kind of person that grows one or two plants for their own use. The choice of what to grow, in these circumstances, is paramount. After all, much time, energy and love will be expended bringing the plant to a successful harvest (maybe six months' worth of hard work).

As mentioned, we only need a casual familiarity with two fancy words in order to understand the big picture. These two words are *genotype* and *phenotype*.

A genotype is a plant's genetic makeup. Curled up tight in each precious cannabis seed is a genetic map or blueprint. Simply put, this inherited set of rules tells the plant how to grow and how to best prosper in order to ensure a healthy life. Just as your personal genetic code specifies that you were born with a certain number of limbs, and a particular eye color, the cannabis plant's DNA may specify fat leaves, sturdy branches and compact buds with long red pistils. On the other hand, the plant's DNA may specify thin leaves, vine-like branches and loose buds with curly pistils. These features are but a few, among millions, encoded by the DNA and passed along from the plant's parents.

The phenotype is how we see the plant express its encoded instructions. In other words, the distinguishing features (as a whole), displayed during the grow.

Here's an example of how this all works: You could plant six Northern Lights seeds from the same parents and get six differing phenotypes. Some may be taller, some may be bushier, some may flower early and they can all have varying scents. Despite the subtleties, the plants will share a common expression: they'll all be Northern Lights. An expert would still identify any of the six plants correctly. Think of it like a family; your brothers and sisters will, in all probability, look and behave differently to you—but there'll be a certain amount of characteristics that you share,

Lovely colored flowers on this hybrid. The dried buds will be vibrant with color.

meaning that most people will mark you out as a family. You are from the same stock, the same gene pool. You are a phenotype: an individual expression of your genetic makeup. But, just like your plants, you are not solely the expression of your genetics. Something else had a hand in defining the way you are. And it's all around you—*right now*.

The Importance of Landrace

Environment is what shapes the way we physically develop and grow into adulthood. It forces our genetics to respond in the best way possible in order to prosper.

A sativa usually grows lanky with lots of room between internodes.

Take a pair of identical twins; let's call them Joe and Freddy. They are identical at birth and barely distinguishable as children. As adults, who have moved away from home and subsequently grown up through differing environments, they'll probably now be quite different people. Joe may have grown tubby, become a lawyer, struggled with ill health, and had three children. Freddy may have remained stick thin and uncannily fit, and become a farmer.

Why should this be the case? Why such varied end results? They were/are genetically identical, but their phenotypes are varied.

The world around us—the climate, humidity, air, toxins, food, stress, lifestyle— forces our genetic toolbox to respond, to adapt to our surroundings, to evolve. We see it with family groups (as above) and entire populations. An indigenous Icelander shares an almost identical DNA tool set with, let's say, someone from Sub-Saharan Africa. However, the Icelandic man will better deal with the sub-zero temperatures of his habitat. The African woman will better handle the extremes of heat in her home region. Exchange the environments and you will cause stress. Given sufficient time though, both will acclimatize, adapt and prosper.

Environment as an evolutionary influence acts over time to allow a species to best fit its surroundings. Over generations, the species flourishes, excels and consistently displays traits that are a unique reflection of this particularly good genetic/environmental match. In reference to plants, we call this "landrace."

Prior to the 1970s, the bulk of cannabis consumed in the United States was imported. Most of it was sativa landrace. Most carried the region of cultivation in the product's name: Panama Red, Acapulco Gold, Congolese Red, Durban Poison.

They all originate from magical locations, so-called sweet spots, environments that dance with the cannabis plant's genetics

The sativa then fills out creating lovely, long, spear-like buds.

in a way that we humans find beneficial and enjoyable.

The sativa dance, fueled in great part by the plants mentioned above, is impressive. It was the fuel for the hippy generation, fodder for the Cheech & Chong movies. It is the perfect example of how environment and genetics work hand in hand. The sativas are an equatorial landrace family, and grow naturally between 30° North and 30° South. Acclimatizing over great stretches of time, these varieties express thin leaves for better handling the hot climate, and can grow over 20 feet tall. They also mature over a long 12 to 22 weeks. Sativas are, by any definition, an outdoor crop. They need heaps of room, lots of sunshine and plenty of irrigation. Such crops are highly visible and difficult to manage, which is why most cannabis was imported, ready-to-smoke, directly from the landrace regions where nature had performed all the work. However, the sativa dance is but one of the cannabis plant's many expressions.

In the very late 1970s and the early 1980s a new kind of cannabis plant was introduced to the West Coast of the United States. Imported from Afghanistan and the Hindu Kush, the plant was landrace but short and stumpy, had fat leaves and matured in as little as eight weeks. This was *Cannabis Indica* (first categorized in 1785 by Jean-Baptiste Lamarck), found prospering at latitudes between 30° to 50° North and South. Just as with the sativas, the indicas' names instantly reveal their geographic origins: Afghani, Iranian, Uzbekistani, Mazar-I-Sharif, Lebanese, Nepalese, Kashmiri, Hindu Kush, Pakistani.

Growers at the time realized that by crossing the indica with the sativa, many of the qualities of each could be retained. The soaring head-high of a great sativa could be retained but mixed with the lower height and faster budding time of the newly imported indica. This first cross would result in a hybrid consisting of 50% sativa genetics and 50% indica genetics. Further breeding— backward and forward—was used to stabilize the resulting genetics, and to push them in the direction desired by the grower/breeder. For instance, a hybrid consisting of, say, 75% sativa and 25% indica may be desired. This is called a sativa-dominant hybrid. The result will be a plant that is predominantly

LANDRACE

Defined by Wikipedia, landrace is: a domesticated, locally adapted, traditional variety of a species of animal or plant that has developed over time, through adaptation to its natural and cultural environment of agriculture and pastoralism, and due to isolation from other populations of the species.

sativa: showing the attributes expected—head-high, light, breezy, maybe thoughtful and intellectual. The leaves will be thinnish (though not as narrow as a pure sativa), and the plant may grow taller than the average indica variety but not as tall as a pure sativa.

On the other hand, switch everything around and you'll have an indica-dominant hybrid: a plant that is predominantly indica, showing the attributes expected—stony-ness, heavy, drowsy, maybe thoughtful and dreamy. The leaves will be thickish (though not as broad as a pure indica), and the plant may grow shorter than the average sativa variety, but not as short as a pure indica.

It is this period in time—when sativa and indica first meet—that humankind's relationship with the cannabis plant created evolutionary paths never anticipated by nature. We began to breed the plant for specific, hybrid-enhanced qualities, previously not seen in the natural world. The human environment, just like all environments, turns the evolutionary crankshaft. The breeding frenzy that started late last century has not stopped. Fast forward to the current day, and there are well over 2,000 distinct strains listed on leafly.com.

Nowadays we are breeding to highlight attributes that weren't even considered a couple of decades ago: auto-grow tendencies, terpene and cannabinoid profiles (specific percentages of THC or CBD), flowering times and the like—all discrete expressions of the plant and all sharing, to some degree, original landrace

Sativa leaves are typically thin allowing better air circulation in hot climates.

genetics. This is an important point. It means we can still gain access to the wonderful genes we need to grow spectacular landrace cannabis, so long as care is taken with seed selection. We may need to wade through the ordinary, the bland, the normal to get there, and we may have to ignore the fashionable—the lemon, purple, berry and gorilla trends—but it all pays off in the end.

Another concern is blandness. Due to the indiscriminate crossing of varieties and competition in the marketplace, the past couple of decades has produced a certain "sameness" across commercially available cannabis.

BREEDING BLANDNESS

In his book, *Cultivating Exceptional Cannabis* (2003), famed breeder DJ Short had this to say about this early period of activity: Never before in human history was so much genetic diversity of cannabis grown in such generic, indoor conditions. The results have literally wreaked havoc on the cannabis gene pool.... As outdoor production diminished, primarily due to intolerant laws (the Drug War), indoor production of indica phenotypes became the staple of the commercial indoor grower. The road to generic blandness had begun.

Generic blandness, as cited by Short, is something that we must—more than ever—be careful to avoid. Artists who work with paint, call the phenomenon the Sea of Grey. It's what happens when you continuously, and without thought, add colors to a mixing pot. The result is a muddy gray every time. Indiscriminate breeding creates a similar greying-out in plants, too. The magical component of the dominant landrace is whittled away, unshuffled and diluted over generations of crosses.

So what do we do to capture the magic for our own gardens? How do we grab some great genetics, the stuff of "potential"? We begin with great seed.

CHAPTER 2

Packets of Potential

Seeds carry genetic code. This will express itself via our chosen grow methods and available environment, resulting in the finished product. The better the seed (its genetic quality and physical integrity), the finer the end result. Our aim is to grow spectacular medicine, so our seeds must be spectacular to start with.

As we have read in the previous chapter, it is the landrace strains that provided (and continue to provide) the genetic recipes for success. The landrace goodness is—to differing degrees— accessible through all varieties, including hybrids. The greater the genetic makeup of any singular landrace strain within the hybrid, the better. Consider the concept of the Sea of Grey once more. If we consider the landrace component as a primary color, then we can reach down into the swirl of genetics and pull out that magic. The plant can then be grown to exploit the potential and to develop the expression of the desired characteristics.

Shop for seeds that consist mostly of the primary hue you desire. Some landrace varieties are still available. If you can acquire any from the table on the following page (and they are worth the effort), then you will have some amazing genetics on hand.

11

Any of these landrace strains will give you amazing medicine—reminiscent of the mind-blowing experiences I salivated over earlier. They will shine with the vibrancy of the primary colors and produce results exceeding all expectations.

Being "landrace" means the plants are best at expressing their magic under specific environmental and grow conditions; something we'll discuss shortly. It may not be possible for you to obtain the landrace strains you desire. If this is the case, the next best approach is to eke out direct progeny—the early hybrid work; the original children of the gods. These were all landrace, crossed with each other (as indica/sativa hybrids or sativa/indica hybrids) in efforts to stabilize and enhance for new grow environments and the attributes loved by humans: potency and flavor.

Crossing short and stumpy indica landrace varieties with tall and unruly sativa landrace genetics resulted in a more easily managed plant. Sativa flowering periods were pulled back from

LANDRACE STRAINS

Sativas

Durban Poison. South African Landrace (Weed.co.za)
Mekong Haze. Southeast Asian Landrace (Delta 9 Labs)
Thai. Northeast Thai Landrace (Original Seeds)
Violet Thai. Ko Chang, West Coast near Myanmar (OtherSide Farms)
Waipi'o Hapa. North Shore, Big Island, Hawaii (Centennial Seeds)
Kilimanjaro. Tanzania (World of Seeds)
Moroccan. Ketama Valley (gibridov.net)
Acapulco Gold. Mexico (SnowHigh Seeds)
Rio Negro. Columbia (Centennial Seeds)
Swazi. Swaziland, South Africa (Tropical Seeds)

Indicas

Hindu Kush. Western Kush Region (Original Seeds)
Mazar-I-Sharif. Mazar-I-Sharif region, Afghanistan (Bomba Seeds)
Afghani. Kush Mountains, Afghanistan (Alpine Seeds)
Lebanese. Beqaa Valley, Lebanon (Alpine Seeds)
Kandahar. Kandahar City, Afghanistan (gibridov.net)

Great genetics deliver results you can see.

12 to 20 weeks to a more manageable 8 to 12 weeks.

Hybridization also meant that the mad head rush of a sativa landrace could, for instance, be tempered with a relaxing injection of indica landrace genetics. Alternatively, an overly couch-heavy indica landrace could be given a little life with some sativa landrace genetics thrown into the mix.

By accessing the early hybrids, you are handing yourself healthy doses of landrace genetics; the genetic profile of the selected seed will consist of almost 100% of a particular landrace. Not 10% of this, 40% of that; instead, you will have in your hands a strain that is 90% Colombian—or, possibly, 85% Thai. Approaching from the indica angle, we might find early hybrids offering 90% Afghani—or 80% Pakistani.

An easy way to dip your toes into this sea of early hybrids (and thus a healthy dose of landrace genetics) is to locate Haze and Kush varieties. These are very early hybrids and form the backbone of many of today's strains. With any Haze or Kush variety you will be acquiring a healthy dose of exciting landrace genetics.

What is a Haze Plant?

The Haze varieties grew out of California when a group of underground growers hybridized a selection of sativas drawn from Columbia, Mexico, Thailand and Southern India. Seeds and clones eventually made their way to Holland and these were the genetics subsequently used for further breeding.

Haze is mostly sativa. It grows tall and lanky. Haze flowers and buds for between 8 and 20 weeks. The effects are heady, cerebral, bright and uplifting. The term high (as in "high in the clouds," or "high as a kite") is used to describe a sativa's effect on the user.

Haze is predominantly (sometimes completely) sativa. The early breeders often added some indica genetics to their hybrids to give the strains a little of a narcotic body-feel (and to shorten flowering times). Some awesome Haze strains include Super Silver Haze, Royal Haze, G13 Haze and Super Lemon Haze. Neville's Haze is especially worth tracking down, as it's packed with landrace genetics from all the key areas: Mexico, Colombia, Thailand and India.

What is a Kush Plant?

The Kush varieties have grown for thousands of years throughout the Afghan/Pakistan regions, along the mighty Hindu Kush mountain range (hence the name). Originally, and still to this day in limited areas, the plants are grown for hashish production. Fast flowering and low growing, the plants are laden (leaves and all) with glistening trichomes during late flowering. Hash Plant and Hindu Kush are examples that still strongly express this trait. Afghani #1 is a cornerstone strain that serves as the foundation for such world-dominating hybrids as Skunk #1, Northern Lights, Sour Diesel, Cheese and even the Blueberry lines.

A young Kush variety, displaying early trichome development.

Kush grows small and bushy. Kush flowers and buds for between 7 and 10 weeks. The effects are weighty, drowsy, heavy and narcotic. The term stoned is used to describe an indica's effect on the user, as in "the weight of stone," or "dragged down like a stone."

Kush is predominantly (sometimes completely) indica. The early breeders often added some sativa genetics to their hybrids, giving the strains some cerebral uplift. Some awesome Kush genetics to explore include Hindu Kush, Burmese Kush, Master Kush and OG (Ocean Grown) Kush.

Taking the above into account, we know that the acquisition of great landrace genetics (and the early hybrids) will result in seeds that are capable of producing extraordinary results.

What is a Good Seed?

A good seed will be healthy, free from disease or inherited nasties; easily germinated and—most importantly—it will contain fantastic genetics. Such a seed has the potential to ensure

Re-sealable plastic balm containers are ideal for storing seeds.

vigorous growth, a healthy yield and the delivery of a sensational end product.

How do we source something with such potential? To obtain great seeds requires a little research and social interaction. The secret is nailing down a supplier who will be honest with you. Someone who will entertain your inquiries when you say you're looking for a landrace; specifically Durban Poison, Mekong Haze, Thai, Waipi'o Hapa, Moroccan, Acapulco Gold, Rio Negro, Swazi, Hindu Kush, Mazar-I-Sharif, Afghani or any of the varieties we discussed above.

These freshly sprouted seeds are ready to be planted.

You need a supplier who truly cares about genetics and has a deep knowledge of their stockholding, someone who will joyfully discuss their range of Haze and Kush varieties. Your source could be a trusted friend, or maybe an associate with an impressive grow history.

If you've found a particular variety that exceeds your expectations at your local dispensary or co-op, then quiz your favorite bud-tender for a source. On the other hand, you could find a mainstream supplier online or in the pages of glossy trade magazines such as *High Times Magazine*, *Marijuana Venture* or *Weed World*.

Before making initial inquiries, be it to a friend or via the online route, there are a couple of further considerations: your grow environment and the strain to suit it.

Grow Environment

The great landraces and the early hybrids—the genetics we desire—all flourish in very specific environments. It is this environmental pressure upon the strain's genetics that has, in part, shaped the end result. These strains are the way they are because of the environments they have become acclimatized to.

The strains mentioned in the previous sections (or any, for that matter) will not perform at their best if grown in an unfamiliar environment. This must be factored into your final seed selection. Can you provide an environment that your plant will feel at home in? The answer is: You must try.

Carefully consider the environs that your chosen variety is

used to. What makes the plant happy? Does it have a sunny disposition? An absence of wet feet? Does it prefer an early sunset? Think about temperatures, photoperiod (the length of the night period), pH requirements, tolerated humidity, correct nutrient requirements, watering rates, pest and disease resistances and strategies, growth height and flowering times. The better you can simulate the plant's preferred environment, the greater the chance of unleashing the pent-up potential. Do your research.

Types of Seed

Back in the old days (that's the period before Spotify), your choice of seeds was very limited. Your only option was a regular mixed pack; a potluck with regards to both the sex and the quality of the seeds. It was normal to get about 60% females and 40% males, although sometimes you'd get shafted completely. Your seed supplier would take your money and offer a cheerful, "Good luck!" Many a bar bet has been won and lost over an individual's apparent ability to distinguish the sex of a seed through visual and tactile clues—something we'll address in the next chapter.

Today, the choice of seed type is broader. Feminized seeds have become popular, as have automatic and semi-automatic varieties. Let's break it down.

Regular Seeds

A pack of regular seeds will be a random mix of female and male seeds. Chance indicates at least a 50% probability of the seeds being female. More often it's 60% (nature has its reasons). Thanks to the mix of sexed seeds, a regular pack may be your best choice if your intention is to breed. You may want, for example, to produce additional seeds of a particular variety, or you may want to create a hybrid to combine attributes you find desirable. In addition, both males and females can be cloned without concern, meaning that cuttings can be taken and grown as separate plants genetically identical to the donor plant. The males and females can also be mothered; that is, they

A sprout pushing upwards, about to discard its hard shell.

Good genetics produce seeds that discard their shells with ease.

The seedling should grow with vigor, just like this beauty.

This bud has been pollinated and is producing its own seeds.

can be held in a permanent state of vegetation by controlling the photoperiod. A pack of regular seeds allows for these future possibilities and these are points that should be considered if you want to maintain a consistent crop for a long period of time.

Feminized Seeds

With a pack of six feminized seeds you will grow six female plants; there is almost zero chance of getting a male. These seeds are created by a process called rodelization, a term coined by a controversial breeder called Soma. It's also known as selfing, and it can occur naturally or be chemically induced. These are seed clones—identical to the parent plant in every way. The all-female offspring will exhibit the same photoperiod sensitivity (and other attributes) as the parent, making them perfect for further cloning if desired. The plant can also be mothered.

Commercial rodelization is performed chemically to encourage the production of male flowers on the female plant. The resulting manly flowers are then used to pollinate other female plants of the same strain. The result? All female seeds with no male DNA to be found.

Automatic Seeds

These are varieties that have a dose of *ruderalis* in their genes. This is a species of cannabis with a genetic profile that specifies age as the flowering trigger. Normally it's the photoperiod change, the lessening amount of light per day, that acts as the trigger for flowering, not maturity (how old the plant is). With the trigger attached to maturity, these "automatic" plants begin to flower at a certain age, say 28 days, no matter how many hours of sunlight they encounter. This results in short plants that have little time to vegetate; once the maturity trigger is reached, flowering begins.

You cannot clone an automatic strain because it lives out its life regardless of the photoperiod. Regeneration is out of the question, too. You cannot keep an automatic variety as a mother. Even under continuous light, these plants will mature and flower. Breeding is not an option.

Semi-automatic Seeds

These are feminized seeds with a smaller dose of *ruderalis* in their genetic makeup. Again, they are small plants that will flower with anything less than continuous, 24-hours-a-day light. Cloning is difficult, but not impossible. A 24-hour photoperiod will keep a plant mothered and offer the opportunity to vegetate—thus adding bulk and new flowering regions.

Once you have decided on a specific strain that you'd like to grow, and when you've considered the grow environment and decided on a seed type (regular, feminized, auto, etc.), you will be ready to locate a trustworthy, reliable and safe seed supplier.

Begin by making inquiries at your local co-op or dispensary. Ask around. Your curiosity will probably be met with enthusiasm and a great desire from others to help.

The next best approach is to look over social media. Join a few web-based magazines and forums; you'll find plenty of lively feedback and commentary about seed suppliers (good and bad). It's probably a bad idea to send DMs to strangers on any social media platform, especially if you're very obviously trying to buy anything that's not legal where you're located. Remember that the internet is still much like the Wild West of yesteryear—lawless and full of hacks. So take care.

Upon locating a seed bank with a reputation that impresses you, a company with a phone number and email address for contact, open the channels—put in the call. See if they are a good fit; discuss your specific requirements with them. You'll soon know if it's going to work out.

RECOMMENDED SEED BANKS

At the time of writing, the following seed banks/distributors are excelling at providing healthy stock, reliable information and prompt delivery:

Advanced Seeds (advancedseeds.com)
Barney's Farm (barneysfarm.com)
Bomb Seeds (bombseeds.nl)
Canna Mana Co (cannamanaco.com)
Centennial Seeds (centennialseeds.com)
Delta 9 Labs (delta9labs.com)
Dinafem Seeds (dinafem.org)
Dutch Passion Seed Company (dutch-passion.com)
Mandala Seeds (mandalaseeds.com)
Original Seeds (originalseedsstore.com)
Sensi Seed Bank (sensiseeds.com)
Serious Seeds (seriousseeds.com)
TGA Genetics (tgagenetics.com)
Tropical Seeds Co (tropicalseedscompany.com)
World of Seeds (worldofseeds.eu)

Seed Management

Whether you have successfully acquired one seed, a dozen or hundreds, you'll need to store for future use those that aren't yet germinated. If you're going through a great deal of trouble obtaining superior genetics, it would be a shame to lose the hard-fought potential through deteriorating seed stock. Luckily, seeds can be kept for over a decade when properly stored.

Your seeds will deteriorate if overly affected by heat, moisture or light. The golden rule is to store your seeds in an airtight container in a cool and dark location. If storing different varieties, place them in small, individual containers. I use small balm canisters. These are easily labeled—with strain information and date—before being placed in a larger airtight and lightproof receptacle. Larger quantities can be stored in those huge vitamin and protein supplement bottles/jars sold at health-food and fitness outlets.

Stored safely in a cool and dry place, seeds will last two to three years, maybe longer. This can be increased to five to ten years by keeping them in the refrigerator, or up to 20 years if you freeze them (and leave them frozen).

An important caveat: If you are intending to store seeds that you have produced yourself, you must allow them to dry sufficiently before sealing them in airtight containers. Failure to do so will run the risk of trapping excess moisture within the confines of the storage canister, resulting in the formation of mold and other nasties. The rule of thumb is to allow about five weeks of drying before storing. It's as easy as leaving the seeds in a cup atop your bookshelf, or in a similarly cool, dry spot.

Sinsemilla: seedless buds.

The bud on the left has mixed seeds. On the right? Probably two female seeds.

Sexing Unknown Seeds

Is it possible to tell if any individual seed is male or female? Are there clues within the seed's color, shape, markings or other characteristics that provide a clue? It's a question that has captured the imaginations of enthusiasts for decades. The correct answer could save you weeks of wasted time vegetating an unwanted male, so it's worth considering.

You will (or rather, you should) know the sex of the seed if you specified it from your seed bank. That's the safest bet! If, on the other hand, a friend has appeared with a single seed and asks you to identify its sex, can that be done? The answer is yes!

Let's say you found a single seed in a bag of brilliant herb. Under these circumstances, the seed will be female. How is it possible to know this? A seed is a seed, right? We can make a good guess as to the sex of the seed by examining it in context— where it was found, for instance, and how many other seeds accompanied it. Let's imagine, for the purposes of explanation, that we have a trio of identical quarter-ounce stashes. The first stash contains *no* seeds, the second stash contains *dozens* of seeds, and the third stash contains a *couple* of seeds.

In the first stash, you have what is called sinsemilla weed (it's Spanish for "without seeds"). This is cannabis deliberately grown to be barren. This is ideal for non-growers, as you are not paying for the weight of a bunch of seeds, and, thankfully, you don't have to pick seeds out of the buds to enjoy the product. Today, sinsemilla is what you expect when you purchase herb. It wasn't always this way. In the 1970s and 1980s, seeded stashes were the norm, and it wasn't unusual to spend time with a shoebox and credit card raking the seeds free and muttering "There must be a better way."

Consider the second stash: you've acquired a nice little quarter of your favorite herb, and at the bottom of the bag (or throughout the buds) are dozens of seeds. These seeds are likely a combination of male and female, or they are hermaphrodites. The grower was, undoubtedly, attempting to grow sinsemilla; they don't want their merchandise filled with seeds any more than you do. So what happened?

The probable scenario is that the plant was accidentally pollinated by a nearby male. Cannabis plants are germinated by wind-carried pollen, and pollination can take place even when one takes great care to avoid it. It may be that just a few buds out of the whole crop were affected and the grower didn't notice. If this is indeed the case, then you can count on the seeds being a mixture of both males and females.

Germinate a minimum of five and you will be able to settle the matter. You can then cull any males and grow the female(s) to full maturity.

On the other hand, a large number of seeds like this can indicate hermaphrodites. These are the result of poor genetics—and/or poor growing technique—producing both male and female flowers on the same plant. This is a very bad thing. Self-pollination is inevitable, and the resulting crop will be full of hermaphroditic seed, making it almost too much of a bother to clean and consume. Again, the germination of five seeds will settle the matter. If they result in hermaphrodites (with both male and female flowers on the same plant) then dispose of all the plants and the seeds. You do not want to pass on these poor genetics to future generations of plants. You will never breed out the hermaphroditic trait. Kill the possibility stone dead.

Finally, the third of our hypothetical stashes. To discover only a couple of seeds in your stash is great news, as they will most probably be perfectly viable females. The reason for this, as we've discussed, is a process known as "selfing." It's an emergency call to arms undertaken by the plant if allowed to over-ripen. When a ripe female cannabis plant is permitted to grow past the final budding period, it sometimes panics and throws out a couple of male flowers; nature's attempt at ensuring survival of the genetic line. Under such

Clear, just from the differing marks, that two strains are present.

circumstances, only a few adjacent female flowers receive the pollen and produce seeds. Because these male flowers contain only female genetics, any offspring must be feminine. You may germinate these seeds and be almost 100% confident that they will be females.

The golden rules: Lots of seeds in your stash means they are either a mixture of male and female, or hermaphrodites. A couple of seeds in your stash means—in all likelihood—that you have female seeds.

While it is always safest to acquire your seeds from a reputable seed bank, great seeds can be obtained from a good stash. According to legend, the jaw-dropping Chemdawg (Chemdog) family originated with seeds plucked from a $500-stash deal purchased at a Grateful Dead concert.

CHAPTER 3

Pillars of Potential

The popularity of gardening shows on TV (and social media accounts focusing on the same thing) highlights the current booming trade that can be done by stores that sell all types of plants, shrubs, trees and soil. The products now available through the resulting plant superstores are uniformly excellent—and a good potting mix is terrific for cannabis.

Soil

If you are a new grower, or live in part of the world without access to high-end, canna-tuned soils from specialized outlets, then I'd suggest using a modified retail potting mix as the basis for a good growth medium. Such a product, available from your local gardening store, will more than suffice and will buffer most nutrient deficiencies—something we'll discuss later.

Locate a high-quality mix with a balance of nutrients and water crystals. These water crystals will assist in retaining moisture between waterings. A premixed soil that boasts 3, 6 or 12 months continuous feeding is what you're after. Hunt down a product that carries a warning about the inclusion of live bacteria (and recommends the use of a face mask); this is a soil that's alive, and your plants will appreciate that. Grab a couple of bags. Don't be picky about the price; good soil is not cheap. The investment, however, is worth it. You're creating a life-support system for your plants here.

You must add perlite to your soil mix. Perlite is a neutral form of volcanic glass—formed by the hydration of obsidian—that breaks up the soil, ensures good drainage and increased air circulation, and boosts overall health. Most commercial soil mixes tend to shrink over time (thanks to the organic filler matter slowly breaking down) which can result in compressed soil around the root mass. The plant's roots will not receive the intake of air between waterings if the root system is smothered. Perlite protects against this by creating a sort of micro-scaffolding that props up the mass of the surrounding material.

Preparing the Soil and Pots

Tip a bag of "living" soil into a wheelbarrow and spread it out. Add perlite and mix it in thoroughly. Your blend should consist of about 75% soil and 25% perlite. When well mixed, the final result looks speckled.

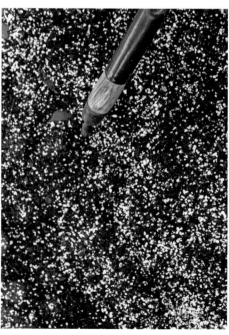

25% perlite to soil ratio.

Mixed through, perlite offers soil support.

Push about ²/₃ of the mix to the side of the barrow, and then add a single handful of granulated all-purpose garden fertilizer to the remaining soil, boosting it with nutrients. Mix this extremely well to ensure there's no clumping.

Load your pots ¹/₃ full with the boosted soil and then place the regular soil on top, filling the pots. The boosted soil will make a nice treat for your plants once the roots have had time to adjust, grow, and search for the nutrients.

A good potting mix and perlite to aerate and support the soil are a must.

Water

Water is a precious resource; the universe's great solvent. Cannabis plants love water that's clean, not too acidic and contains no chemical nasties. Most growers will not have access to fresh stream water, tank water or groundwater. Tap water is what we usually have to contend with. To make the water "safe" for mass consumption it's often treated with chemicals. Chlorine is a popular choice; it's used to control bacteria that may otherwise contaminate the water supply.

Warning label indicates live bacteria and advises precautions.

Unfortunately for our gardens, this very same chemical will kill the vibrant hub of micro-organic life flourishing in the soil that we have carefully chosen and prepared. To allow our plants to reach their potential, we need to assure good, healthy water— we need to eliminate the chemical component and then address the acidic balance (pH). Making sure you have these things covered will allow your plants to acquire the full benefit of the nutrients in the soil mix. Here is how to prepare tap water for use with cannabis plants.

Eliminating Chlorine

Shops selling aquariums have a product to make aquarium water fish-safe. Its primary job is to dissolve the chlorine that would otherwise kill any fish introduced to the environment. However, if you have 48 hours up your sleeve, there is another way—we can trade time for chemicals.

Chlorine evaporates over time; this is why pool owners have to continuously replenish it. Therein lies the key to simple, no-cost de-chlorination. By filling large buckets with tap water and leaving them in the sun for two whole days you will allow the chlorine to dissipate, and other unwanted elements in the water will sink to the bottom of the bucket.

After two days, carefully decant most of the water into fresh buckets. The 10% remaining in the original buckets will contain sunken debris (including some heavy minerals, if present). Now that the water is chlorine-free, it's time to check the acidity level.

Getting the pH Right

"pH" is a term used to describe the acidic level of a solution. It's a logarithmic scale, measuring hydrogen ions. At room temperature, water with a pH balance of 7.0 is "neutral." That is, it's neither acidic nor alkaline. Acidic solutions have a pH reading of less than 7.0 and alkaline solutions have a reading over 7.0.

Cannabis, when grown in soil, has the potential to excel when the pH is held at an average of 6.5 to 7.0 throughout the growing and flowering periods. Anything higher or lower than this will make it difficult for your plant to absorb the nutrients it needs from the soil. This is something referred to in the botanical field as "nutrient lock out." Symptoms can include stunted growth, discolored/twisted leaves, wilting and death. If you are growing hydroponically, a range of 5.5 to 6.5 can be better suited.

To ensure your plant's health, you must keep the pH levels of your water and soil within the required range of 6.5 to 7.0. The first step: buy a pH meter or a pH paper-strip test kit. If you are adding any sort of nutrients to the water, execute the pH test after you've added the food. Nutrients can shift

Baking soda and lemon juice, your pH adjusters.

the acidity of the water in unexpected ways. Be aware that changing seasons, drought and unexpected heavy rain can affect the pH balance of your local water supply. With all these variables to consider, it is important to test the pH of your water *every* time you water your plants. No exceptions. I once lost a whole crop through a sudden pH shift following heavy rains.

Use the apparatus of your choice (an analogue/digital electronic tester or color-strips) to read the pH of your now de-chlorinated water. If the pH level fails to fall within

Analogue pH meter. This model works with water and soil.

the desired parameters, use very small quantities of commercial pH adjusting juices (generically know as "pH-Up" and "pH-Down") to bring the reading into line. Alternately, if you are dealing with only a few buckets of water, lemon juice can be used to lower the acidity and sodium bicarbonate (baking soda) can be used to raise it. Use very tiny amounts of either to make the adjustments. Retest the pH between each corrective action and repeat if required.

Never water your plants with cold water. Always let your water settle at ambient temperature. Never over-water your plants; cannabis does not do well with wet feet. It's a good idea to allow pots to fully drain by propping them on an angle with a little wedge or pebble.

Lighting and Environmental Concerns

Lighting has always been a bone of contention with growers. Many will swear that growing outdoors is the only way to reach full potential; others will tell you that it can be done indoors with artificial light. Both, of course, can be considered correct.

That being said, it's probably a better time to be growing outdoors than it has been in a while. With the lifting of prohibition in many countries, states and territories around the world, it is becoming legally safer to once again tread outside into the light. There is simply less chance of being locked up. It was prohibition, after all, that forced growers indoors.

Our plants will enjoy the gradual move back outside into the natural sun with its full spectrum of goodness. It all just seems more natural, organic and planet friendly. Let's hope the trend continues, because commercial use of electricity (most of it created via burning fossil fuels) is growing at an alarming rate, to the detriment of the planet.

Power usage in states like Colorado went through the roof upon the legalization of cannabis. Some estimates even put the total national usage of electricity by the cannabis industry at between 1% and 2%. That's huge!

The massive power usage within the cannabis industry is explained by the use of HID and HPS grow lights, fans, air conditioners and the like—all designed to keep the environment inside a grow space at its optimum. HID and HPS lights create huge amounts of heat, wasting energy in the process and requiring even more energy usage to keep the grow room the desired temperature. There are massive greenhouses running these lights—plus the required air-support systems. The rush to keep up with the new and legal demand for cannabis is pushing power requirements past a comfortable zone. Again, most of this energy is being provided by burning fossil fuels. It will take decades before alternate energy sources are efficient enough to support demand. As an example, today's best solar panels (on average) are about 16% efficient; this is why you need so many of the things on your roof. The day will come when solar, wind (and other alternates) will carry the burden and lessen our reliance on fossil fuels.

In the meantime, as small-time growers caring for a couple of plants and growing our medicine of choice, we can (and must) do our part to reduce our carbon footprint. The easiest and

The cost-efficient luminance of an LED light.

Natural vs Artificial Lighting

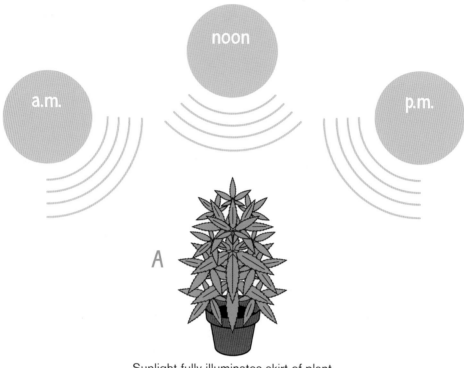

Sunlight fully illuminates skirt of plant

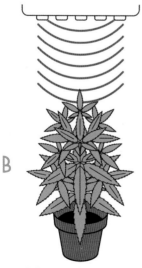

LED only illuminates
top third of plant

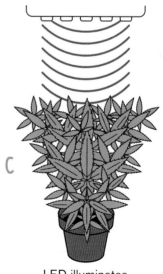

LED illuminates
entire "flat-top" plant

most efficient way of saving power—one that benefits both the environment and one's pocketbook—is to grow outdoors whenever possible.

This is made clear in the diagram, which displays various lighting configurations. Note how (in part A of the illustration) the plant can receive light over its entire surface. As the sun moves across the sky, the plant's skirt is bathed all round and from head to toe. Such depth of light penetration is to be desired, but can only be encountered outdoors.

Single and four-panel LED lights from Hydro Grow.

Indoors, under even the best LED light, the plant—when left in its natural Christmas tree configuration—will only receive quality light at the apex. (Part B of the illustration.) To use LED lights efficiently, we must train our plants with flat tops to better interface with the light. (Part C of the illustration.) Later, we'll spend quite a few pages looking at how to best do this. The benefits are strong: LED lights are ideal for both vegetative lighting (18/6 or 20/4 or 24/0) and the flowering cycle (13/11 or 12/12). They use a minimum of electricity, creating almost no heat and saving energy by eliminating the need for fans or air conditioners.

Furthermore, the argument that LED lights do not provide an adequate light spectrum for the production of fine cannabis has been disproved over and over. I've disproved it myself. LED lighting has become a mature technology; what were once considered "toy lights" are now the environmentally friendly lights of choice for growers of all levels of skill. The plants grown for this book, my previous book and dozens of my magazine articles have all been grown outdoors or under LED lights. So, make the switch to LED and help reduce the industry's carbon footprint.

CHAPTER 4

Advanced Techniques & Know-How

If you are reading this book, it should come as no surprise to you that there is a lot of nuance to growing marijuana. While some might view gardening as a simple equation (sunlight + water + soil = healthy plant), growing your green is far more complex than that. This chapter is all about the techniques to help you maximize your plant's potential.

The Best Way to Germinate Seeds

This is the best goddamned method EVER for seed germination, and I mean it. Once you try the technique described, I doubt you'll ever go back to the old wet-paper-towel approach. It's the first time this new method has been documented in any grow book, making it a wonderful start to our initial section about advanced techniques. Successful and consistent germination depends upon addressing the following parameters.

Seed Viability

Your seeds need to be fresh and healthy. They should not be green in color, as this is a sign they lack maturity. If you intend to grow flowering plants, your seeds should be female—something you can be assured of by ordering from a reputable seed bank, or by applying the "sexing" rules previously discussed.

Once you have ticked these boxes, decide how many seeds you would like to germinate. I'd suggest a minimum of three (or five, if you have the available stock). This way, even if the sexes are mixed, you should (statistically), end up with at least one female plant.

Temperature Parameters

Cannabis seeds will germinate if the temperature is between 70°F and 80°F. Maintaining a consistent temperature is key. You need to find a spot in your facility to allow this. Fluctuations—forcing the temperature beyond the specified sweet zone—will severely affect your results. Sudden drops in temperature can occur at night, so think ahead; prepare for all contingencies.

Moisture Control

The precise delivery of water to the seed is where most problems arise when using the traditional wet-paper-towel technique for seed germination. The beginner is often so excited

A teaspoonful of water beads goes a long way.

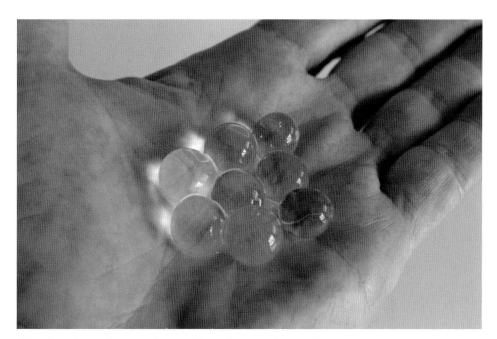
Clear beads are the best to use; they allow you to see the action.

to see their first seeds sprouting that they'll constantly check the paper towels, disturbing the seeds and interrupting moisture transfer. This often leads to germination failure.

The seeds must receive the right amount of water allowing the "meat" of the seed to rapidly expand, cracking the outer shell. If the uptake of water is too slow, or is impeded (by constantly disturbing the paper towels) then this rapid expansion and cracking of the shell will not occur; the seed will die, having expended all of its energy trying to break free. On the other hand, if too much water is available to the seed it will drown once the outer shell cracks.

Ideally, we need an automated system; something regulating the precise amount of moisture delivered, to ensure not too little but not too much. Exactly what is the correct amount of water that needs to be delivered to the seeds? The answer is: whatever the seed requires.

The solution is to use a product called water beads. Also known as water pearls, jelly soil, dragon eggs or water gel, they are made of a polymer known as SAP (Super Absorbent

Shooting visible after just a day or two.

Polymer). They absorb water, swelling to many times their original mass when they are soaked. The photographs show how a small quantity of beads, soaked in water, swells to fill a bowl.

The truly amazing thing, and the real benefit to the germinator, is that the spheres are now able to release their water content at the exact rate your seeds require. Via a process similar to osmosis, the seeds, while resting against the spheres, draw the water they need at the rate they need it. As this process is automatic, you no longer have to worry if the seeds are too wet or too dry for germination to occur. No longer do you have to peel apart layers of wet paper, disturbing the seeds, in order to check their status. In fact, by using clear water beads in a clear glass tumbler, you can see exactly when the seeds germinate without having to disturb them in any way. Hands free, baby!

Here's how to do it:

First, source a little pack of water beads from your local florist, wedding planner or market stall. They're not hard to find and can be ordered online if that's easier for you.

Place about a teaspoon of beads in a small bowl. Fill the bowl to the top with pure, filtered water (or bottled water) and soak for between four and six hours until the beads are fully bloated. Then pour off the surplus water.

Half fill a clear shot glass with the expanded beads (as in the photograph).

Take, let's say, three seeds. Drop them into the shot glass so they sit separated from each other on the swollen beads. Gently spoon sufficient beads into the shot glass to completely cover the seeds. Refill the shot glass about halfway (no higher than the level of the seeds) with the clean, room-temperature water.

You need only place the shot glass in a warm (70°F to 80°F) environment to allow germination. I like to invert a coffee mug over the shot glass, keeping the seeds in the dark as they don't need any light at this point. The seeds will draw just the right amount of water from the water beads. It's automatic and self-regulating.

Check the progress after 24 hours. You'll be able to spot

Half-filled with water beads, this shot glass awaits seeds.

Seeds sprinkled atop the water beads.

germinated seeds (without disturbing them) thanks to the clear sides of the shot glass. If there are no signs of germination, check again at 36 hours and then 48 hours. The photographs show a successful germination at 24 hours.

This is now the only way I germinate my seeds. It's easy, clean and results in near perfect germination rates. I can't say it's 100% effective, because nothing is. What I can say is that this method has never failed to produce germination for me—ever. Give it a go. I know you'll be amazed.

Bedding Down with a Taproot Tunnel

It's time to bed our newly germinated seeds for their initial growth. As with the process of germination, this is a sensitive time for your plant. The seeds have expended most of their energy getting that first root out. A comfortable environment is what they need now if they're to become healthy children, ready for vigorous adolescent vegetation and to unleash their potential. (Vigorous adolescent vegetation; now there's an oxymoron.)

An important consideration for seedlings is the development of a solid taproot. Healthy roots mean a healthy plant, and the taproot is the foundation upon which the plant's entire root system is supported.

Use a deep pot right from the word go. Many people plant their seedlings in tiny pots and then re-pot in several stages. Personally, I believe this puts the developing root system at a disadvantage, introducing stress and potentially stunting growth. For a starting pot, use a deep pot that is at least 20cm to 26cm in depth. The deeper the taproot can plunge, the larger the early root ball will be. More importantly, the plant will have the opportunity to fill out the available space without the interruptions of repotting.

Soil and Temperature Requirements for First Growth

The all-purpose soil mix described in Chapter 3 is perfect for use here, and in fact at all stages of the plant's future growth and development. Later, during vegetation, we may want to supplement with a little nitrogen, and at the onset of flowering, a boost of potassium and phosphorus. We'll discuss this later.

Perlite, seen here as white specks, helps keep the soil aerated and healthy.

Poking a hole all the way to the bottom of the pot with a steel skewer.

Gently placing the sprouted seed—root first—into the preformed hole.

Tamping the seed, ensuring it is just covered with soil—just.

After a day or so the plant pushes its head through the top of the soil.

The first pair of "true leaves" forming with vigor.

Temperature must also be considered when bedding down the sprouted seeds. Cold feet or overheating will stunt growth at this early stage. The ideal temperature range, as previously mentioned, is between 70°F and 80°F. Be aware that sudden drops in temperature can occur at night. Never place pots on the floor. Floors can become frosty.

Potting Procedure for First Growth

Let's get these babies growing! Begin by short-filling a pot with the soil mix so that it's only 85% full. Leaving 15% of the pot's depth empty, aka short-filling, creates a built-in shield for wind-sensitive seedlings.

Water the pot (with our treated water, see Chapter 3) thoroughly; you should have visible runoff at the bottom. Allow the pot to drain.

To assist the taproot in traveling unhindered towards the bottom of the pot, make a tunnel with a skewer or slender stick, no thicker than a match. Push it into the soil in the middle of the pot, straight down, all the way to the bottom. The resulting channel must be thin, no thicker than the seed itself. You don't want the seed falling down the hole.

Now, using a pair of sterile tweezers, gently grasp one of your sprouted seeds by the shell. Feed the root into the hole you've made in the soil. Stop when the upper tip of the seed is flush with the soil. Gently tamp down with your finger, ensuring no more than

After a week or so we have three sets of leaves—a happy plant.

1mm of soil now covers the seed.

Do not water at this point; to do so runs the risk of compressing the soil and restricting the seed. Instead, maintain a moist environment by covering the top of the pot with Saran wrap. Stretch this taut and then secure it with a rubber band. Thus prepared, the pot will behave like a miniature greenhouse. Short-filling allows room for the seedling to sprout properly—the plant has wiggle room, something it would not have without that 15% breathing space at the pot's top.

Lighting Considerations for First Growth

Seedlings are best cared for indoors, under artificial light. Even if you intend to grow outdoors, it's best to get the plants started inside where they will be out of the wind, away from a scorching sun and free from pests. As previously mentioned, I have had great success with LED lights. However, even fluorescent lighting will work for the early seedling stage.

Place the pot under continuous light. Be sure that the temperature will be maintained within accepted parameters. After 48 hours, carefully peel away the plastic cover and check your seed. If you see nothing, replace the plastic cover, return the pot to the light and have a look the following day. By now, you should see the seed breaking through the soil. It may or may not have shed its shell. Never be tempted to physically remove a clingy shell from the cotyledons (the first leaf emerging from a germinating seed). It will drop away in time.

At this stage, the pot and seedling no longer require the greenhousing, and the plastic cover can be disposed of. Maintain the emerging plant under continuous light for the next two weeks.

A pair of "true" leaves will emerge from between the cotyledons within days—you'll recognize them by the tiny serrated edges.

Do not apply nutrients at this point. Your soil is rich enough. Water, air and light is what your babies desire right now. Try to adjust the height of your lights, moving them up and down, so that the new leaves are well lit and angle upwards slightly towards the light. If they are flat, or drooping, then your seedlings are not receiving sufficient lumens.

Weather permitting, you can boost the available light with natural sunshine. So long as it's not windy, seedlings just love the warmth of the real thing.

After two weeks, your seedlings should have grown up to four sets of leaves. The plant will have grown past the rim of the pot and should be standing strong, proud with potential.

Inoculating Against Pests

Pests come in many shapes and sizes. A pest is anything that poses a threat to your crop or your well-being and safety. Next to deficiencies in the basics (soil, water, pH and lighting), pests pose the biggest threat to your plant's future potential to excel.

Large pests include dogs, cats, rodents, foxes, wolves, even kangaroos—it all depends on geography. Most of the damage threatened by the above pests (trampling upon or consumption of your plants) can be prevented with a chicken-wire fence and basic precautions.

Humans too, can be pests—especially if they rip off your lovely plant(s). The first rule to securing your grow from human pests is not to tell anyone about your grow. Do not brag to friends. Do not be tempted to offer anyone a grand tour of your grow room or facility. If anyone knows, then security is breached. Even a friend may turn into an inadvertent pest. Beware.

Smaller pests can circumnavigate the fence, flying or crawling into your grow space. Such pests can include lizards, locusts (grasshoppers), moths, whiteflies, spiders and ants. Any of these nasties would like to munch on your plants to varying degrees. Many are seasonal, only appearing when the environmental circumstances are favorable. Locusts appear at the same time each year; the youngsters are disguised just like leaves and quite hard to see. They are best picked from your plants manually and then squished between a thumb and finger. Do it before they reach adulthood!

Other pests are capable of introducing infestations that can wreak havoc. You do *not* want to deal with these later—they must be nipped in the bud at the very first sign. Here are some particularly nasty guests that your plants can encounter.

Aphids. Among the most common problems a cannabis

Scary stuff! Guys like this can devastate hectares of crop.

grower can face, these nasties are introduced to your plants via ants. Aphids suck sap from your plants, weakening them. They then excrete honeydew, the ants are rewarded and the cycle of destruction continues.

Leaf miners produce larvae that are hard to see but damaging nonetheless.

Scale is related to the aphid but they become hard little shells upon maturity. They almost look like bland-colored ladybugs; little sap-sucking terrors they are. Pick them off by hand; this is easy enough, so long as you catch the infestation early.

Spider mites. Hope that you never encounter such beasts. These guys are tiny, come in the millions and can completely destroy a plant in two to three days. If you see web-like fluff surrounding your buds, then it's probably too late.

Many other dangerous liaisons also await the unwary gardener—lacewings, wasps, whitefly and thrips—but fortunately, we can prepare in advance. A little foresight goes a long way when considering pest control and the health of your plants.

Signs of damage, like this partly eaten leaf, demand your attention.

The first thing to consider is the hygiene of your grow space. Keep all debris clear, as it can harbor bugs. Likewise, do not allow soil, grow medium, rags or containers to gather in the grow area. Incoming air (if you are using a circulatory system) should be cleaned at the point of entry. Stretched-out nylon pantyhose (sheer stockings) make an exceptional filter material. Always clean the grow area from ceiling to floor with disinfectant between each grow.

Spiders are mostly harmless and just "passing through."

The absolute best trick I've ever learned for overall pest management—and plant health—is to inoculate your plants. The simple process (administered during the vegetative stage) will prepare and protect your plants through the flowering and budding periods. By inoculating you are preventing infestation by most pests before it can start. As I've already said, once you notice an infestation it's probably too late to do anything about it. So, planning ahead is a no-brainer.

Inoculating your cannabis plant is as simple as spraying it with an amazing plant-based product called Neem oil. Classified as a vegetable oil, it is extracted from the fruits and seeds of the *Azadirachta indica*. Grown on the Indian subcontinent, this plant's oil has been used medicinally, and as a biopesticide, for over 5,000 years.

The extract acts as a phagorepellent (antifeedant) and blocks the molting hormone (ecdysone) in many insects. Simply put, Neem oil forms a lovely shiny coating on your plant's leaves that makes them totally noxious to most pests. It does this without blocking the cannabis plant's stomata (the microscopic pores on the plant's epidermis) that allow gas and moisture transfer and are essential for photosynthesis.

By treating the vegetating plant every 14 days—until it reaches the point of beginning to flower—you will protect the plant, keeping it pest-free and healthy so that it may blossom with vigor.

How to Inoculate Your Plants

First, purchase a bottle of Neem oil. It's a tad expensive but it's normally applied as a very mild solution, so it lasts a long time. Store the oil in a cool place between uses. Consider this an investment in your plants' health. I promise, you'll be thankful later.

How to Inoculate Your Plants

1. Grasp the plant loosely and sweep upwards following with the Neem oil spray.

2. Continue upwards, following with the spray, wetting the leaves' undersides.

3. Finish by dousing the tops of the leaves to the point of runoff.

Obtain a spray bottle capable of emitting a fine mist. Mix in a quantity of oil and water per the instructions on the bottle. Typically, this is 5ml of oil per 1L of water. Shake well and the solution will go slightly milky.

Your plants are ready to begin the process of inoculation once they're about two weeks out from germination. The aim is to saturate the plant (including under the leaves) to what's known as "runoff." This is the point at which excess liquid is dripping off the plant.

Gently grasp the plant around its base. Form a loose ring around the base with your fingers and thumb. Now raise your hand slowly up the plant as you follow with continuous squirts of spray from the bottle. Repeat three more times, rotating the plant a quarter turn between each run. This ensures a full wetting down of the leaves' undersides.

Finish by dousing the tops of the leaves from above. You'll know when you've reached runoff as droplets will be forming on the leaf tips. At this point we can be satisfied that the plant has been completely cocooned in the diluted Neem

An incidence of the pest known as "scale." Get rid of it and keep an eye out for more.

Can you spot the single egg on the underside of this fat indica leaf?

Holding a leaf up to the light is a great way to check for insect damage.

Not all bugs are troublesome. Ladybugs eat aphids! Good girls.

oil. Give the pot a quick shake, snapping the plant back and forth, shaking free all the excess liquid that you can.

Allow the plant to dry in the shade. Be sure it gets no sun until properly dried. Failure to pay attention to this will result in sunburn that will manifest as brown, burned patches on your leaves. I like to leave the treated plant in the shade for at least a full day.

Repeat every 14 days until the plant begins to flower—but only until it begins to flower. Do not under any circumstances spray Neem oil or an insecticide (of any kind) on a flowering plant. You will eventually be consuming the flowers, so you want nothing to have contaminated them—*nothing!*

Surefire Cloning: Nub and Rest

The term "cloning" seems a little highbrow, sounding more scientific than it needs to. Cloning is, in reality, nothing more than taking cuttings. People do it with all sorts of plants, and have done

Early training—tipping—has produced many shoots suitable for cloning.

Water, potting tray, scissor and "rooting powder" ready for cuttings.

so for eons. It is possible to take many cuttings from a single plant and turn all of these into a small farm of identical plants.

Plants struck or cloned from the original plant are identical to the mother plant (and to each other). They share the same attributes, the same DNA. They also share the biological age. For example: Take clones from a plant that is just about ready to start flowering, and the cloned (and regrown) plants will be ready to flower as well. They are all the same biological age. Of course, by maintaining a 24/0 photoperiod you can grow them into larger plants. They'll pop back into flowering once you reduce the daylight hours.

The fact that you can work up a whole farm's worth of identical plants from a single mother plant is incredible—but true. The system allows you, for instance, to preserve a specific strain, keeping it alive and thriving season-in, season-out. By keeping a healthy mother plant, cuttings can be taken repeatedly for years. Some of the world's best and most exclusive strains are available as "clone only." In other words, you cannot buy the seeds; you must either purchase or be gifted a clone from the mother plant.

How to Take Cuttings

1. A target branch. Cut below the leaf node.

2. The removed branch with lower leaf node intact.

3. Cut the lower leaf away leaving just a nub of plant matter behind.

Another use for cloning is to "test-flower" a plant to establish if it is male or female. To do this, take a clone from the plant you are unsure about, establish it and then force it to flower by changing the photoperiod. The main plant continues to vegetate. Once the clone shows its sex, you can decide what to do with the mother (or, perhaps, father) plant.

Other benefits of cloning include the opportunity to distribute cuttings of a specific strain to fellow horticulturists and the ability to save a pest-infected crop in an emergency.

The ability to take successful cuttings is a great tool to have in your box of tricks, allowing you to preserve and further propagate plants displaying the desired potential.

Let's look at how to take these cuttings or clones in a consistent and successful manner. Like many other techniques, a little practice makes perfect. There are a couple of guidelines and a trick that will make this process more likely to be successful. You will need:

- sharp scissors
- a glass of water
- rooting powder (or gel)
- small pot(s)

A tray of clones ready to begin their new lives.

Ensure your scissors are sterile and that the water is pH-balanced. You don't want to introduce any bacteria or create any shock. Rooting powder is available from most garden supply stores. It's a hormonal growth enhancer sold specifically for the purpose of making the rooting of cuttings easier. If using the powdered version, be sure to wear a face mask. You do not want to be inhaling stray hormones.

Preparation

Prepare your small pots, one for each cutting you intend to grow. Use the same soil that the mother or host plant is growing in. Again, we are trying to avoid shock. Water well and then drain off. Finally, poke a hole into the center of each pot by using a pen. It is into this hole that you will plant the fresh cutting.

Making the Cut

Your mother plant should be healthy and growing with vigor. Using your scissors, cut a healthy and vigorous branch, just below a leaf

node at about halfway down the branch's length. Immediately drop the cutting into the glass of water so that air cannot enter the cut. Such an air bubble, otherwise known as an **embolism**, is often fatal and the most common cause of clone failure.

Now here's the trick I alluded to earlier: You will make a second cut. Carefully snip off the lower leaf, but leave behind a little nub. By retaining this bump (where the leaf joined the stem) you create a much greater chance of the cutting actually "taking" and then rooting.

Quickly, again to avoid embolism, lift the cut section out of the water and poke it into the hormone powder. The powder will cling to the cutting around the cut area. Make sure it's a smooth coating and not clumpy. Immediately poke the cutting into the pre-formed hole in your grow pot. Tamp down the soil to hold the cutting secure.

A successfully "rooted" cutting.

Repeat for as many cuttings as you require. However, you should never harvest more than 20% of a plant's growing shoots at any time. This can cause stress. Let the plant recover for two weeks before taking further cuttings.

I can't overemphasize the import of leaving that little bump of material intact. For many years the process of cloning had given me trouble, but this tiny finesse has solved the problem, ensuring a near perfect hit-rate.

Allowing for Rooting

Patience is the key when it comes to taking cuttings. The cuttings must be placed under gentle and continuous light (such as fluorescent light) and

First flower. Always a magical moment.

then left undisturbed. You must not touch or handle them in any way for at least two weeks. Don't be tempted to toy with them; any movement or disturbance can damage the beginning stages of new root formation.

If the cuttings need water during the recovery period, use a tray that will allow the water to soak up into the pots. Do not water the clones directly.

Keep the plants warm and out of the breeze. If you live in a very dry climate then you may need to cover the cuttings with a large plastic dome in order to maintain a sufficiently humid environment.

Check for progress after about two weeks. You are looking for the formation of tiny new leaves at the top of the cutting. Once this occurs, you should find that the cuttings have begun to develop their own root systems. Once they have "taken," you can repot into larger vessels.

Flowering vs. Budding

Both male and female cannabis plants have a flowering phase; the male flowers in order to produce pollen, the female to receive it. We'll discuss the male flowers in more detail later. For now, let's look at the flowering cycle of the female plant.

Typically, female flowers appear white (or amber) to the human eye. The flowers' fluoresce, produces enticing images in the insects' slice of the light spectrum. The female plant also makes itself inviting to passing pollen-carriers by producing the sticky balls of liquid that cover the flowers and the areas around the flowers. Known as **trichomes**, these glands bulge with the plant's active ingredients and terpenes, giving the planet the distinctive aroma and flavors we so love.

Early flowers at two weeks.

Many consider cannabis flowering and budding to be a single stage of the plant's development, but I've always considered them as a pair of distinct phases: flowering *then* budding. They are separate episodes, each having a clearly defined beginning and ending. To fully reach its potential, the plant has to pass through this flowering stage—and into budding—so that the quality of the active ingredients and the bulk (yield) of the plant are optimized.

A good "bloom" additive will get flowering off to a flying start.

Flowering

Flowering is initiated by a change in the photoperiod. In nature, this occurs as winter settles in and the long, hot days of summer become shorter. If growing under lights, you will trigger the change in photoperiod with the use of a timer; alter the light regime of the vegetating plant to 12 hours of light followed by 12 hours of dark. This is known as a 12/12 photoperiod. It should be noted that it is also considered an *average*. Some plants prefer a slightly shorter day, some a slightly longer. There is about an hour each way that you can play with in order to tweak the final results. Does the strain prefer a slightly longer day, with the resulting shorter dark period? Some do. By growing the same plant through several generations you'll be able to fine-tune this, thus bringing out the potential in the strain.

This onset of a longer night period forces the plant to alter its hormonal makeup, triggering the floral response. The plant begins by showing us just a single flower. It is a moment to rejoice, confirmation that it's a female. It's at this point you can feel that happy glow—knowing a bounty of sweet and fragrant fruit lies ahead.

During this time, it's a good idea to tweak the nutrient balance so the plant is receiving less nitrogen; it needed more during vegetation, but not so much now.

Instead, to help with strong and vigorous flower development at the beginning of the flowering stage, the plant could use a boost of potassium and phosphorus. You'll find a suitable product easily at your local gardening store. Look over the nutrient breakdown on the side of the packaging; what you want is categorized as a "bloom" product (as opposed to a "grow" product). Use sparingly.

Flowers in abundance at six weeks.

The flowering has finished. Note the hundreds of white flowers.

Initially, apply at half the manufacturer's recommendation to avoid burning or shocking your plants.

Over the ensuing weeks, the plant will fill out, throwing out thousands of pairs of flowers (**stigmas**) until it is covered in bunches at the grow tips and along the stems. In the photographs alongside this section we can see a Mullumberry (Mullumbimby Madness/Strawberry Cough) plant filling out over several weeks. The flowers multiply and stand proud.

Typically, a flowering period takes about four to seven weeks. At the end of the period you should have large and fluffy flower heads. Don't make the mistake, as many novices do, of thinking that this is a ripe plant. It's far from it, even though the plant may be glistening with trichomes. This is the end of flowering and the *beginning* of the budding phase.

Budding

Budding is what happens when flowering has finished. It is also the period during cultivation when the grower must show the most patience. To be impatient at this point is to lose potential yield.

The process of budding occurs in the last few weeks of the plant's life. The pretty flowers begin to retract and some die, turning dark brown, orange, or even red. The reproductive pod at the base of each pair of stigma also begins to swell. This is the place where a seed would form if the plant had been pollinated. The photographs alongside this section show a bunch of flowers before budding, with the bud having begun to swell, starting to engulf the tired flowers.

This swelling will continue for a few weeks (three to five, depending on the strain), and the flowers will become *less visible* as the buds add bulk. The difference in weight between an unripe (not fully swollen) and ripe (fully swollen) bud can be 200%. You can more than double your harvest by being patient and allowing your buds to fully swell.

Where does this extra bulk come from? Good question. With the bases of thousands of flowers bulging in unison, each retracting its flowers, there's a proportionate increase of surface area. When the cannabis bud swells it can actually become

Nice sativa bud and ball of hash made from the sugar leaves.

quite solid, the bloated false–seed pods pushing against their neighbors and stretching the structure taut. Depending on the strain, a solid bud can be as hard as a golf ball. A lumpy surface area is greater than a flat surface area. Nature uses the same trick across many plants, animals and even inside us humans: the surface areas of our lungs (and our brains) are vastly increased with this folding trick.

From the grower's view, the greater the surface area (the more lumpiness), the greater the quantity of medicine. Simple as that. A well-ripened bud is fat and covered with trichomes. Most of the flowers have been engulfed by the expanding mass. The golden rule: if you see masses of flowers, your plant has not finished budding. A ripe bud is almost bald.

Bud of Mullumberry.

Is the Plant Ready Yet?
Throwing Out the Rules

Having passed through the flowering phase, the plants can technically be thought of as budded. However, this may not translate immediately into them being ready to harvest. To be sure we're ready, there is a final check; the trichomes are the key, the deciding factor.

Traditionally, at this point, the author of a grow book will direct you to locate a small magnifying glass. In today's day and age, we all carry a perfect alternative called a smartphone. The cameras in the latest devices are fantastic; you can take a photo and then zoom in to such a degree that the individual trichomes are easily seen. (See Chapter 8 for further photographic suggestions.)

Close up, under your digital magnifying glass, trichomes look like tiny mushrooms; each with a thin stalk supporting a ball of liquid on top. Inside each of these are the plant's active ingredients, passing through several stages as the buds mature.

In the early, non-mature stage, the trichomes look clear and contain the precursors of our beloved tetrahydrocannabinol (THC) and its roughly 113 supporting cannabinoids. Along with this, terpenes and entourage elements are also developing. Note that trichomes appear to be clear during most of the flowering and budding stages. It's only toward the late stages of bud maturation that these tiny globes begin to change color.

Early indications of change are when the trichomes begin to turn cloudy. They will do this by passing through a translucent stage where you can still just see through them. Soon, depending on strain, the little balls will become slightly cloudy. A week or so later they will cloud up further, becoming almost white. This is a sign that the plant is approaching maturity and that the THC has almost fully matured. At this point we are approaching the traditional window of harvest. Most of the cannabinoids and precursors are fully formed and at their most potent.

Left a little longer, the trichomes will begin to change from cloudy to a gentle golden hue. This a sign that the THC has fully developed, and is beginning to break down into CBN. As the trichomes continue to turn gold (or brownish) the THC continues to break down, drastically altering its psychoactive effects.

It used to be a rule, almost set in stone, that you *must* harvest when the trichomes are beginning to turn (or have mostly turned) golden. It was almost blasphemous to consider harvesting anything other than mature, fat and bald buds, just this side of deceased, with their golden hue and diminished THC profile. Golden buds were considered the peak of potential.

Nowadays, with the ever-broadening body of cannabis knowledge and a greater availability of cannabis to legally purchase, it has become apparent that the grower can deliberately alter his harvest to create a medicine to suit specific needs. We see this a lot in the field of medicinal cannabis: carefully sourced varieties being grown and harvested at precise times (according to the trichome profile) in order to address a particular medical condition. Harvest early for one type of medicine, harvest late for another.

As we have already discussed, an indica plant tends to create a stoned feeling while a sativa plant tends to impart a high. The clever grower, by watching their trichomes, can control the effect their plant offers—dialing it in to suit their needs or desires.

By harvesting an indica plant early, when the trichomes have just turned cloudy (or are about to turn cloudy), you will ensure that the resulting crop is far less stoney and much more "active" than the typical indica.

At the opposite end of the scale, if you allow the trichomes to turn fully golden, the narcotic tendencies of the plant will be fully realized. We can also tailor a sativa plant so the end result will reflect our specific needs.

I've already mentioned a variety known as Mullumberry (early cut); she's almost all sativa, consisting, primarily, of long-inbred Thai and Columbian genetics. At 12 weeks (84 days) of flower/budding, she's sensational. But at just 54 days (way too early, some will scream), she's transcendental—the closest I've been able to get to the beloved Thai sticks of yesteryear. Sure, by harvesting ¾ of the way through the cycle I'm losing yield, but it's worth it. Pure magic. Potential realized!

When you are growing for yourself, you can break the long-held rules in any way you want.

Lovely buds, glistening with trichomes.

Experiment in order to find the budding period that encapsulates your favored experience. Finding this sweet spot only requires a willingness to experiment, a systematic approach and something called the calibration bud.

The Calibration Bud–Part 1

The calibration bud allows you to dial in the exact medicine you want: pain-relieving, antidepressive, feisty, dreamy, razor-sharp; your choice. This is your opportunity to maximize the plant's potential in the potency and flavor stakes.

The calibration bud also has another useful property: it can make accurate slow-drying of your crop an automatic process.

First, let's examine how we can fine-tune the plant's spectrum of available medicinal options. Used in its traditional way, taking an early sample or performing a "taste test" was undertaken solely to determine ripeness prior to harvest. A bud, snipped from the plant, was flash-dried in an oven allowing for an immediate assessment to be made. It has always been understood that flash-drying is *never* a good idea, with delicate flavors burning off and the nasty taste of chlorophyll being amplified. However, a ballpark judgment certainly could be made by an experienced grower; someone capable of mentally subtracting the noise. (We discuss this further in chapter 6).

By using the above concept in an ordered and systematic fashion (most definitely avoiding the flash-drying bit), we can accurately map a plant's changing profile as it progresses through the prolonged period of flowering/budding. This will allow us to explore a particular strain's potential across its entire blooming cycle. What we learn can throw up a whole smorgasbord of medicinal qualities, flavors and experiences.

An indica plant offers about one month's worth of differing medicinal profiles, all accessible with the calibration bud (weeks 5, 6, 7 and 8). A sativa plant offers about five weeks (7, 8, 9, 10, 11 and 12).

For the purposes of determining the very best time to harvest a plant, especially a coveted specimen that you intend to spend serious time with—either by regeneration or cloning—I would

This wet calibration bud weighs in at 1.68g.

suggest taking a calibration bud at each of the aforementioned weekly markers.

Each time you take a sample, select a bud that is not too large (you don't want to shortchange yourself by lopping what will eventually be a very substantial cluster) and not too small (it needs to be a fair and good example of what the plant has to offer). A good, small-to-mid-sized bud is what you are after. You'll find something suitable about a third of the way down from the top of the plant.

Snip the bud from the plant and, if you wish, trim off any leaves not covered in trichomes. Before you set the bud aside for slow drying, grab a set of digital scales and weigh this freshly harvested bud. Write down the wet weight and keep the note. In our photograph the wet weight is 1.68g.

Slowly dry the bud by placing it in a small paper bag and then

leaving this in a cool and well-ventilated spot, or simply place it in a cup and leave upon a shelf in a dark and well-aired room.

You will know when the bud has properly dried by giving it the classic snap test. Do this by bending the bud at its midpoint. If the stem snaps, rather than just bends, then the bud has sufficiently dried. You should actually feel the decisive snap; you may hear it, too. It is the section of stem within the bud that we are talking about here, not the bit of stem extending out the bottom.

Finally, weigh the dried bud. Write down this dry weight beside the previously recorded wet weight. For the record, the dry weight of our calibration bud was 0.35g. The difference between these weights is equivalent to the water lost during the process of drying. We'll put this data to good use in part two of the calibration bud discussion, drying by weight, in Chapter 6.

Once the calibration bud has been properly dried, it can be put away for a later taste test. As you progress from week to week, store away each bud with a clear label indicating its age (*Week 5, Week 6*, etc.).

Weigh the fully dried bud and take note of the water lost during the drying process.

After finally harvesting the plant you will have sample buds, all properly dried, which can be tested over the course of a week. You'll take a journey through the entire spectrum of what your plant has to offer: early THC precursors, THC maximums, THC breakdown and all points along the path. A noticeable characteristic is the difference in scent and flavor between weekly points. The terpene balance certainly shifts. My beloved Mullumberry (early cut) has the most delicious floral scent (at seven to eight

To test for dryness, bend the middle of the bud, not the protruding stalk.

weeks) which is compromised when the plant is allowed to fully mature at 12 weeks.

By the time you get to decide if your six or seven-week-old calibration bud is the winner, your plant will have fully matured. This means that you can only apply the procedure to clones or regenerations of the original donor plant (something you will have addressed early in the grow cycle). Use the information gleaned from your calibration buds to harvest your next batch of flowering clones (or regenerations) at their recently discovered relevant sweet spots.

CHAPTER 5

Vegetating for Potential

Training is a process by which we can extract the greatest potential from a plant in terms of yield and potency. Maximizing growth patterns through good training encourages additional shoots to form, which in turn develop into additional budding sites. Our aim is to get the plant to interface with our light source in the most energy-efficient way. Light is the food of potential.

As we have discussed previously, if left alone to do its own thing, the cannabis plant will form a large single cola (central growing stem) with much smaller side branches emanating from it in the typical Christmas tree growth pattern. It's fine to leave such a plant to do its thing in the great outdoors—but inside, under lights, or in a pot in the back garden, the plant will require careful attention and training to reach its true potential. A sativa needs to be tamed and bushed out to create width instead of height, and an indica needs to be bushed out to create greater yield. By creating a bushy plant you are maximizing the canopy, the umbrella of top leaves that intercept the most light. The greater the canopy—when it consists of additional growing shoots, each

73

aching to become a cola—the larger the yield. Your seed has the ability to grow into a plant the size of a car, so let's release its pot-bound potential! If growing a sativa strain, you'll have to be very careful of limited ceiling height, as they can grow very tall.

To achieve a truly bushy plant requires training from an early stage—very early. This is something that used to be frowned upon due to a fear of stunting growth. We now know that this is not the case. A vigorous F1 seedling will just love the chance to branch out and become lush as early as possible. I recommend getting straight into it from the appearance of the third leaf set by using the processes of tipping, training sticks and super cropping.

First, though, here is a crash course in the technique of regeneration—an example of the amazing potential that can be unleashed with the right know-how. It's a technique that we can use over and over to maximize yields and to preserve our favorite strains.

Regeneration: A Primer

Even though I penned an entire book on the subject of regeneration, the process is such a profound expression of the cannabis plant's potential that I feel compelled to briefly revisit the topic here.

Top colas jammed together. Training creates the freedom to develop unhindered.

Simply put, regeneration allows you to rebirth, regrow and re-flower the same plant over and over. In other words, if you have a particular plant that you just love to bits, regeneration gives you a chance to grow the exact same plant again and again! Sounds impossible, right?

The regeneration of anything—be it a plant or an animal—is a miracle of nature; something that can launch religions, cultural and

A regenerated bud producing lots of new growth.

Regenerated buds are identical to those grown from seed.

scientific revolutions and even genres of fiction. Yet, strange as it may seem, regeneration or the spontaneous return to life does actually occur in the plant world. And, luckily, it's not scary at all—just beautiful, as can be seen in the photograph alongside this section. This bud, regenerated, is in the early stages of regrowth.

Regeneration occurs with particular ease in the genus *Cannabaceae*. That's fortunate for us, the cannabis lovers. Indeed, if you've been a proponent of the plant, whether recreationally, medicinally or just out of curiosity, then you've probably come across the terms re-green and re-vegetate. These are both terms for regeneration. Surprisingly, the very same information on the subject has been circulating since I began investigating it decades ago. The consensus has always been that regeneration is a technique best reserved only for emergencies; moments like saving a precious plant when you've neglected to take seeds and clones.

I have suggested (and proved with my book) that regeneration can be much more than this. I believe this magical spark of life can be harnessed, captured, trained and finessed into a complete grow discipline; a system that allows the user to regenerate the same plant over and over, producing up to 100 medium-sized buds per cycle. At the same time, the technique saves power, space and time.

But what about the results in terms of quality and yield? What do regenerated flowers and buds look and taste like? Are they mutant or strange in any way? No, they are just the same as any other flowers or buds—genetically identical, in fact. Many of the plants and buds photographed throughout this book are regenerated specimens.

How Regeneration Occurs

The cannabis plant is an annual plant. This means it's genetically programmed to live once and to die hard over a single season. The plant has evolved, hand in hand with nature's influences, with just a single goal before dying: to produce seed.

The process by which the plant enters its important flowering stage (ready to receive pollen, and to then produce seeds) is initialized by hormonal fluctuation as the amount of the day's available light contracts to about 12 hours.

The trigger required to reverse this process, stimulating new growth (regeneration), is a return to a solid 20 to 24 hours of light per day. Such a period is not available to the plant when it's preparing to die in the natural world, during its 12-hour slumber (harvest time). For this reason, I think it possible that regeneration of the cannabis plant could not have evolved as a grow option until the advent (due to prohibition) of growing beneath artificial lights. Regeneration is therefore a latecomer to the options we have for growing. So, how is it done? How do you regrow and re-harvest the same plant more than once?

My system was intended for the medicinal grower needing just one or two plants of consistent quality, but it can equally be upscaled by the recreational grower who may be allowed to grow 6, 9 or even 12 plants.

In this primer we'll learn the basic technique of re-harvesting an existing plant in a single pot, bringing it back to life and producing lots of good buds in the process.

A regenerated plant stripped so you can see the amazing growth pattern.

A treated plant, ready to be regenerated.

The beginnings of regeneration. New growth sprouting.

A couple of weeks later and this regenerated plant is ready for training.

The first step is the selection of a suitable plant to regenerate. The specimen needs to be plump and ripe, ready for harvest. In addition, if we are to regenerate, there must be a couple of buds low down on the main stem. Everything above this point is harvested with a single chop and hung upside down to dry in the traditional manner—slowly.

Once the chop is made, and the harvest is hung, the remaining stump needs to be treated as if in Intensive Care. Time is critical: during this period the plant's compromised vascular system must be stabilized. It's roughly comparable to an animal's cardiovascular system; however, unlike the arteries, veins and hearts found in animals, plants are filled with lignified tissues (xylem) for conducting water and minerals throughout. Your plant's waterworks are shot at this point, needing attention. The wound must be dressed, protecting against embolism or bacterial infection. Using gaffer tape (or a hot-glue gun), seal the open wound. Trim the extreme tips from any remaining buds to encourage new growth and then return the plant to a continuous 24-hour light source. With attention to pH, nutrients and temperature (things you've learned from the plant's first grow

A trained canopy creating a flat interface with the light source.

cycle), regeneration will occur at least 90% of the time.

The initial signs of success are magical, appearing anywhere between 4 and 14 days from the cut. As you can see in the photographs here, the old calyxes begin to regrow, pushing upwards on tiny stalks. Truly a miracle. Think about it: just a few weeks ago these old calyxes had been waiting for pollen. Now, rebirthed, they begin regenerating as leaf matter. These first leaves don't even look like typical cannabis leaves; they're bereft of jagged edges and smooth. These are "emergency leaves"—something the regenerating plant sends forth as urgently required solar panels. The ornamentation, it seems, can wait until later.

With the successful saving of the harvested plant, the flurrying buds will produce about six grow shoots each. Assuming two treated buds, that's 12 new shoots.

It's worth noting the speed of this. If you had popped a seed at the same time you had regenerated your plant, would the germinated seedling offer you 12 or more healthy growing tips? No, it would not. You'd have a single stem and one or two sets of proper leaves, that's it. In comparison, regeneration is *fast!*

The secret to getting the most from regeneration is to train these shoots into a horizontal spread, forming a flat top. This ensures that all the growing shoots will receive equal light. It's this efficient interface that allows us to grow so many buds in a single pot, under a solitary light. The full vegetative cycle—the time it takes the plant to fully develop its flat top—will be about 38 days. During this time, exposed nodes will develop, reaching upwards for the light. They will eventually flower and then bud.

The flowering cycle will last about eight weeks or so depending on the strain. Throughout flowering and budding, it is only necessary to undertake minor defoliation to ensure that light penetrates deep into the canopy.

The result can be stunning: lots of bud! Money, space and time is also saved with this process. What's even more exciting is that you can harvest your regenerated plant and then repeat the process again. Yes, you can do it all over—and over! See my first book *Cannabis Regeneration* (Green Candy Press, 2016) for further details on maximizing the potential of regeneration.

Tipping for Increased Yield

A seedling, germinated and potted as per the instructions earlier in the book, should, after two or three weeks, have between two and four sets of leaves. These should be "proper" leaf sets, not including the little cotyledons that led the plant out of its shell.

The seedling will have grown well past the rim of the pot and be standing strong on its own. At this early stage, it is advantageous to begin training, the aim being the creation of as many bud sites as quickly as possible. It is easier and less stressful for both plant and grower to vegetate a plant into shape, rather than forcing it into submission later. Tipping is one of the tricks we can use to create additional growing sites by creating a bushier plant. If we intend to interface the plant with an LED light then we'll be aiming at a flat-topped bushy plant.

Here's how to "tip" a plant. The photographs here show a nice indica with three leaf sets and a healthy central growing tip. Grab a pair of tweezers, making sure it's properly sterilized. Gently bend the side leaves away from the main stalk so that you can

A seedling—with as little as three sets of proper leaves—can be tipped and trained.

A nice indica, ready to begin training.

Locate and then pinch out the tiny growing shoot right at the top.

The growing shoot has been removed.

Two new nubs can be seen forming at the same spot after a few days.

After a week or two, the nubs will be growing as fully independent branches.

eyeball the growing tip at the top of the plant. This is the tip that would, if left alone, grow into your plant's main cola.

Using the tweezers, nip the growing tip completely off. I know that's easier said than done, but don't be afraid. Your plant will recover, and she'll do it with a bonus grow tip. Within a week, two new nubs will appear, growing in the original tip's place. They will develop into a pair of independent branches.

If you treat each new growing shoot on the plant (even secondary growth) with the tipping process you'll very quickly (over two to four weeks) develop a bushy plant with the majority of the budding sites at the top. In order to hasten the procedure, strap down the newly growing tips once they sufficiently lengthen. Pulling them to the side, forcing them into a horizontal stance to better interface with the light, will require the use of training sticks, conveniently described in the following section.

The astounding way that tipping broadens a plant's potential yield is expressed in the numbers. Complete plant tipping multiplies the growing shoots, doubling the size of the plant, with *each* application (1, 2, 4, 8, 16, 32, 64 or 128 growing tips).

Tipping will create many growing shoots and a broad, flat canopy.

Another important benefit of tipping is that it temporarily boosts development at the area immediately below the tipped point, encouraging further growth.

The technique can also be used in a strategic fashion, allowing lower branches additional time to catch up with taller siblings. Remember, we want a nice flat interface with our light source. We are tipping to increase volume and to concentrate growth at the top of a broad canopy.

Eventually, however, the plant will refuse to play ball, reaching its genetic limit or a strong desire to flower. You will recognize this point when the new tips start forming in a stepped formation rather than opposite each other, which is how they normally appear. Indoors, with LEDs, this cutoff point is usually at 64 or 128 tips depending on the strain. Outdoors—well, the sky's the limit.

Making and Using Training Stakes

The most common question I'm asked about training stakes is this: How long are they supposed to be? There is no correct answer. This is why I never specified a length in the description in *Cannabis Regeneration*.

The right length is whatever length is required to do the job. What size pots do you like to use? The depth of these should be a guide as to what length the stakes should be.

Mostly, you'll find the required skewers come in a 30cm length, and in a packet of 50 (sometimes 100). They do the job for small, potted plants. They are supplied in a very thin version (for making little meat and veg skewers to cook over hot coals or on a grill) and a thicker version (for heftier kebab-type applications on an outdoor barbecue). Either will do; just make sure they have pointy tips so that they can slide past and through root masses without ripping and tearing them along the way.

In addition, you'll require a bunch of plastic or wire twist ties. Paper twist ties are best avoided as they tend to deteriorate long before a plant is ready for harvest. You can use gardening wire instead, cutting it into short, 8cm lengths.

Twist a tie around the blunt end of a single stake, then repeat until you've made up the whole bunch. Then, to hold the twist ties firmly in place, apply dabs of glue from a hot-glue gun. Repeat until you have a whole set. Prepare at least 24 at a time (I'd suggest 36).

Tips for Using Training Sticks

1. Use training stakes to bend and pin down branches growing out of your tipping regime. Bend the branch into place and insert

the stake alongside it. Tie off the branch with the twist tie. By doing this you are allowing any secondary growth to have equal access to light. This additional light, in turn, encourages this secondary growth. The circle of life.

2. Try to insert training stakes so that the pointy tip is aimed towards the middle of the pot's bottom. In other words, insert the stakes at an angle. This creates a type of brake, preventing the flexed branch from pulling the stake up and out of position. Remember, a cannabis plant is always trying to reach up towards the light.

3. If your pots are small, then you may need to cut the training stakes down in size, shortening them. Do so with a solid pair of scissors, and then re-whittle the sharp point on the remaining length of stake. Of course, it is always better to think ahead and make any adjustments at the stakes' blunt ends prior to gluing the twist ties in place.

A bunch of prepared stakes ready for the hot-glue gun.

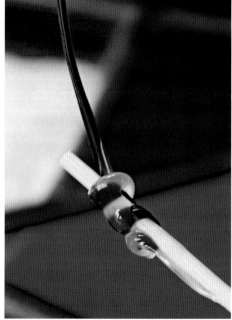

Using the hot-glue gun, secure the twist ties to their stakes.

Plants in need of training.

This plant has been successfully tipped allowing the lower branches to grow.

Staking the first branch. Note the angle of the stake, creating a brake.

All branches staked out allowing secondary growth to proceed upwards.

4. Always insert a training stake slowly and use your sense of touch. If you feel any resistance from buried root matter, then stop. Pull back. Never force a stake; you'll only damage the roots. This may not become evident for a few weeks, until you suddenly notice part of your plant dying off! You can always readjust; pull back and then shimmy the stake along beside (or around) the obstruction. Do so gently.

5. Use training stakes with abandon. You'll soon find that you can use more stakes than you initially made up. That's okay; go and make some more. As you continue to tip your plant and apply super cropping, you'll have many more fresh growing tips than you could have ever imagined. This is your plant trying to reach its potential and a sign that you are doing things just right. The plant's healthy and happy.

6. Training stakes can be used over again for multiple grows. Disinfect between each use by soaking overnight in a 10% solution of hydrogen peroxide. Dry them in the sun.

The staked plant beginning to fill out.

Staked to the extreme and paying off with a healthy yield.

A branch, super cropped, and bent towards the plant's perimeter.

The branch has healed and the elbow, albeit bruised, has done its job.

Super Cropping

Sometimes nature just runs ahead in leaps and bounds; growth spurts can happen at any time and for seemingly no reason. You may have been ultracareful with your tipping and staking, creating a nice and bushy plant with a nice even top, only to later discover a few athletic branches outgrowing the others. Super cropping is a technique developed in order to tame these runaway branches.

A secondary application for the technique is physically halving the size of whole plants that have grown too tall. Used in this fashion, super cropping reduces the size of the plant and at the same time increases the size of the canopy. It's a handy trick to have up the proverbial sleeve, especially if growing lanky sativa plants.

"Brutal" is how some describe the mechanics of super cropping. No doubt, it certainly falls into the category of high stress training (HST), as does tipping. Super cropping is indeed stressful, but mostly to the grower and not the plant. We like to treat our plants with gentle love and care, so applying the technique for the first time can be nerve-racking.

During this process you are going to bend branches over

sharply, at 90° angles. The bent or crimped area will bruise and swell. It's not going to be pretty. Anxiety may settle in as you wait a couple of days to see signs of recovery. But sometimes you have to be cruel to be kind, and that's what super cropping is all about. The plant deals well with the trauma, releasing a hormone that boosts growth in the injured area, often creating denser flowering. The principle benefit is a more efficient interface with the available light. The end result? Healthier plants and larger, more potent yields.

When to Super Crop

Always begin any training program, including super cropping, as early as you can in the plant's vegetative cycle. Once flowering has begun, it's too late. This applies to tipping, staking or super cropping equally. We'll begin with the technique applied to evening out the top of a canopy.

How to Super Crop

We'll assume that your canopy is in pretty good order and that just a solitary branch has outgrown the others. Find a spot on the offending branch somewhere below its main growing tip. This should be at approximately the same height as the balance of the

Another example of super cropping and a healed "knuckle."

The plant's crown presents a single growing tip to an overhead light source.

plant you'd like to match.

The branch needs to still be fairly pliable and not overly woody. Nip the branch firmly, at the point at which you want to fold it, between your thumb and forefinger. Squeeze tightly, trying to crush the internal fibers without damaging the outer sheath. It is always a good idea to have your fingernails trimmed nice and short beforehand. You don't want to rip, tear or penetrate this outer sheath. Wiggle back and forth a little until the spot is compromised and weakened.

Now, at the softened point, bend the branch over to 90°. Be smooth and non-hesitant about this. Don't panic if the bent spot splits a little. Your plant will survive. The bent section should stay at the 90° angle. If it doesn't, then you have to again loosen the joint by gently wiggling back and forth, and then re-bend. Don't be afraid—your plant will survive the damage.

Over the next few days, bruising and discoloration will appear at the bent spot. In time, this area will swell and form a knuckle of sorts. This gives the branch additional strength and the bud material above

Tall, skinny plant will be bent in half to control height.

A good idea to "stake" the bent trunk to prevent it from straightening.

Dowel rods used to crimp trunk.

The recovered plant with its bent trunk exposed.

The plant now presents a canopy of many growing shoots.

A solid flat-top, well vegetated and ready to begin flowering.

A super cropped, staked and tipped plant ready to grow into a productive flat top.

will grow large and healthy; the repaired branch is now reinforced and able to support the extra weight. By super cropping offending branches outwards, away from the center of the plant, you are allowing better light access to the middle foliage and flowers.

Super cropping can also be used to radically reduce the height of an overgrown plant or a plant threatening to grow too tall. As an example, the little plant in the photograph alongside this section needs repotting. Without training, the plant once repotted is going to grow to at least six to eight feet in height, way too big for the designated grow space. It will grow too high, becoming unmanageable, if we do not intervene.

Here it is of great importance to consider our light source. An overhead view of the plant displays only the crown. This is where

HEALTHY VEGETATION

Basic Considerations

Producing a healthy and multiheaded plant requires more than just careful training; more, even, than tipping, staking and super cropping. We need to have the basics dialed-in to support the vigorous growth.

1. Ensure plenty of light. Your vegetating plants require at least 18 hours of light per day; 20 is okay. Plants need a little rest every day. It is important for healthy development. Exceptions to this rule apply to both cloning and regeneration, as discussed elsewhere.

2. Do not over-water. Always allow your pots to run off. The root system is healthier (as are your plants) when the roots are on the march, seeking water and nutrients—pushing through soil, looking for moisture and goodness. Never leave your pots sodden.

3. Protect against pests and disease. Follow the previously suggested Neem oil treatment regime (see Chapter 4) so that when you enter the flowering cycle, your plants will be inoculated. Check your plants every day, or every other day, to make sure they are healthy.

the plant is illuminated by an overhead light source, with the side foliage and the secondary growth being starved of lumens. Super cropping will solve these concerns by halving the size of the plant and offering greater foliage-area to the overhead light source. In this instance, we will be more severe, bending the main trunk and not just a couple of branches.

Considering the age of the plant, it's likely that the trunk will be too hard to pinch between fingers and thumb. Under such circumstances, hefty branches and trunks can be "scored" by employing a couple of short dowel rods. Using the dowels like a clamp, squeeze the trunk firmly between them, creating a deep crimp. Execute this at a point on the trunk ¾ of the way down from the top. A couple of fine splits, if anything, may result. We've already discussed this, and have confirmed that it is not a matter for concern; the plant will recover just fine.

To finish, gently bend the trunk over and secure it at a 90° angle by using a training stake. The stick acts like a crutch, providing support against wind and other unwanted movement as the plant heals. The stake will also prevent the plant from straightening itself out, something it will want to do over the ensuing weeks.

You can see in the near photographs how the procedure has allowed the plant's secondary growth to reach up towards the light source. The main cola is now developing over to the side, no longer hogging the lumens. A much greater percentage of foliage, including the forming buds, is now presented to the light.

Training allows us to grow more medicine with very little effort. When it comes to growing in pots, a well-trained plant, one having its potential more fully tapped, can deliver two to three times the yield of a plant left to do its own thing.

The Versatile Pot Assembly

The Goldilocks Zone is what astronomers call the Earth's special orbit about the sun. Our planet is the perfect distance from the sun, keeping us cool but not freezing and warm but not overheated (well, not naturally anyway). Water, which we need to live, can exist in a liquid state. It's the perfect, comfortable balance.

In order to flourish, our plants must also exist within their own comfort zone. Light, water, aeration and temperature are all important parameters that need to be factored in. Look after these things, beginning with the all-important potted root mass, and your plants will have the extra potential needed to excel. We discussed the basics in Chapter 3 and will now look at some advanced potting considerations. These techniques further enable our plants to live healthy lives, with more opportunities to explore their potential.

Let's get our bearings. Consider, for a moment, the ramifications of isolating a plant in a plastic pot. It's a solid barrier, completely encapsulating the rooted regions. Even the plant's electromagnetic connection with the planet is interrupted. Isolated from the Earth, its environment is now very much finite.

As gardeners seeking prosperous plants, we must make the effort to ensure that each is rooted in its own Goldilocks Zone.

The versatile pot assembly (VPA) addresses the problems of pot insulation (it keeps the root mass cool on hot days), pot elevation (it keeps the pot off the ground ensuring good drainage and pest control) and watering. The VPA facilitates a deep and thorough watering (sucking in a whole lot of oxygen), even covering your ass for long-term self-watering when you're on holiday. The VPA is cheap, easy to locate and assemble, and practical to use.

To institute this system, I use a 20L white pail, and a 14L black pot. You will find something equivalent at your hardware or gardening superstore. The important things are that the pot slips easily into the pail and the lip of the pot settles over the rim. It should sit loosely, preventing the pot from falling into the pail. In other words, they should nest together.

Why is it important that the pot be black, and the pail white? It's because the only good thing about any stock black plastic pot is that black prevents light transmission. The roots of your cannabis plant do not like light. They like a dark environment. This is why you never see roots at the top of your pot. They dive for the dark.

On the other hand, the problem with a black pot is that it is prone to overheat in the sun. Black pots in the sun are not good for root health; they're a major cause of plant failure. This brings us to how the VPA can, as an assembly, be used to provide superb insulation to keep the roots cool.

White pail and black pot that can be assembled to achieve various results.

Pot nested within pail creating an insulating barrier of air between the units.

The Insulation Nest

Here's how we can solve the problem. Our large pail is white. White reflects light. That's what we want. If we nest the black pot within the pail, the outer white plastic will reflect a substantial amount of light and heat and what does penetrate will encounter the inner black pot. As we've learned, the black pot will not allow light to penetrate it. The void between the outer pail and the inner pot creates an air barrier. Air is a great insulator. Growing in the VPA can keep your soil up to 15°F lower than using a freestanding black pot.

Elevation

The ground in your garden is prone to temperature fluctuations at night. Too cold and your plants will stress; it's even possible for the roots to freeze. The VPA answers the call by conveniently keeping the plant well off the ground. This is an important consideration for indoors as well. Your plants should be elevated where possible. Next time you are looking at pictures of large indoor grows you'll notice that the plants are all elevated on stands or tables for the purposes of temperature and pest control.

Deep Watering with the VPA

Proper watering of the cannabis plant is a key to good overall health. The roots need access to water, but must not be left submerged or sodden. An overly wet environment restricts oxygen and can result in root rot. At the other end of the spectrum, if the medium is too dry, the result will be plant-wilt (severe dehydration) followed by eventual death.

A moisture level between wet (but not sodden) and dry-ish should be your target. Allowing the soil to dry out a little between waterings encourages the roots to search out water. They do this by growing, stretching out. It is how the root ball expands to fill the space available to it.

The secret to a good watering is what's called bucket or deep watering. This method ensures a thorough soaking of the soil matter, and the evacuation of excess water also creates a vacuum, sucking air into the soil. It's like the plant taking a great big breath of fresh, oxygenated goodness.

Properly drained, the pot will be perfectly watered; the roots will be happy to draw nutrients as they need them and content to interact with the soil matter. It's a great technique for aerating your roots on a regular basis.

Begin by filling the pail about 80% of the way with water. Then, carefully float the VPA-potted plant in the pail. It will bob about, displacing its volume like an ice block in your drink, and the water level will rise and possibly overflow. Top up the pail so that water at the very top is *just* dribbling over the rim.

The potted plant will gracefully bob back and forth, gradually sinking as water permeates its drainage holes. This may take a couple of minutes. Be patient. Allow gravity and fluid dynamics to do their jobs.

When the pot settles on the pail's rim (in the nested position) then it is almost completely saturated. Observe the soil around the plant's base. Once water breaks through the soil's surface, the pot is considered fully watered.

Without delay, pull the pot straight up and out of the pail. You'll meet with considerable resistance as the vacuum created below will suck air through the pot. This is great news for the roots; a

Pot floating—displacing its volume—slowly sinking into the water.

Pot sinking further, its rim about to nest upon the pail's upper rim.

With water breaking through at the base of the plant, the process is complete.

real breath of oxygen.

Set the pot aside, propping it at an angle with a small wedge or stone. You want to encourage complete runoff. Many pots, it seems, have a nasty habit of hosting a small pool of water at their base. Call it a design fault. Tilting the pot, as described, ensures complete drainage. After a few hours, the pot will be properly drained and can be returned to its spot in your garden (or under your grow light).

Depending upon the climate in which you grow, and what temperature and humidity you're dealing with, deep watering will only be required once every week to 10 days. In the cooler months you can safely go two weeks without watering. Learn to know when your pots require watering by familiarizing yourself with their wet and dry weights. The difference is substantial. Another trick: If you ever see the lower leaves of your plant beginning to wilt (not actually wilting but looking like they are about to), then it's definitely time for a watering.

Medium-Term Self-Watering with the VPA

There are times—some intended, some not—when you may have to leave a plant to fend for itself. It may be a holiday, or you might be moving house or starting a new job; there can be many reasons for the hiatus. During times of extended absence it is important to maintain adequate light and water. Light is the easy fix. Watering, on the other hand, can be problematic. Dried-out pots are the most common cause of plant-death-in-absence (closely followed by spider mites). The VPA can easily be configured to water a plant for up to six weeks, depending on climate extremes. This is plenty of time to take a holiday, move house or start a new job.

With a tape measure or ruler, measure the depth of your VPA pot. In the photograph beside this section, the depth is about 26cm. Take the tape measure to the pail and, using a waterproof pen, mark the pot's depth. This will indicate your maximum water height for self-watering.

Locate a roll of crepe bandage; it should cost no more than a couple of dollars from a pharmacy. It's the stuff you dress wounds with. Alternately, tear long strips, about 5cm wide, from an old cotton sheet or tablecloth. If you cut four strips, each about 90cm in length, you'll have what's needed.

Thread these cloth strips through opposing drainage holes in the base of your VPA pot and cross them over. They should hang from the drainage holes like tentacles. Pull them through so they are all the same length.

Measuring the depth of the pot to establish water-level for pail.

Marking the measured depth onto the pail. This becomes the maximum water level.

Crepe bandage—easily located. Alternately, use strips torn from old T-shirts.

Bandage crisscrossed through the pot's drainage holes. These cloth wicks will absorb water from the pail below.

This plant will be happy—and watered— for several weeks as the grower travels.

Add soil mix to the pot and plant as normal; the cotton appendages will hang below the pot and into the VPA pail, out of the way, until we need them.

To prepare for a hiatus, firstly deep water the plant, giving it a good head start; drain and then refill the pail to the maximum water height we alluded to earlier, and which we marked on the pail. Nest the pot into the pail so the tentacles fall into the water reservoir. The VPA nest will keep your plant watered via the wick effect for at least a month and up to six weeks.

Can this be used to slow feed nutrients? The answer is yes—if the plant is vegetating. A mild nutrient mix is a good idea, to keep up the nitrogen level. I would only use water, myself, if the plant is flowering or budding.

This is a good method to use when necessary, but it is important to know your strain and do your best to avoid long absences in the middle of a grow.

CHAPTER 6

A Potent Harvest

The newly legal cannabis industry has become super serious as it grapples with varying state-by-state compliancy legislations regarding both the medicinal and recreational use of cannabis. You can see this whole new level of professionalism and attention to detail right across the industry. From beautifully conceived retail dispensaries offering customers a comfortable, professional and informative environment through to the high-end packaging and labeling of cannabis products. Behind the scenes, compliancy rules and regulations are often so tight that every single leaf has to be accounted for. Same with every liter of water, every dose of nutrient and every kilowatt of power.

The plants themselves look better than ever too. Browse a recent issue of any cannabis magazine and you'll see beautiful buds. Great-looking plants instill confidence, implying that the grower has prepared his medicine with care and attention to detail. Medicinally, this is very important. Commercially? It's about bag appeal.

For the small-time hobby grower, it's about pride—and medicine that soars high above the average. What does it take to create beautiful buds? They must be perfectly dried. They must yield an exotic aroma upon handling. They must smoke cleanly, leaving a pure white ash. What does it take to achieve this? It begins, as it always has, with drying the harvest—slowly.

The Importance of the Slow Dry

My kitchen, and possibly yours, has a bunch of herbs hanging in a cool corner. In my case it's rosemary, thyme and lavender. The old-school, traditional reasoning for hanging bunches of herbs upside down is to facilitate slow drying and to minimize handling. Attention to both helps us achieve a finer end product: cooking herbs that taste better, smell better, act better. These practices apply equally to cannabis.

Why is Drying Slowly so Important?

The proper drying of our plant is paramount to obtaining the very best medicine. Dry too quickly and the final result will taste and smell "green," the true flavors and scents not having had the chance to stabilize, leaving the plant's chlorophyll too obviously abundant.

On the other hand, drying too slowly has a downside, with the possibility of mold arising. Once this nasty fungus raises its ugly head, your crop will be quickly ruined unless you take emergency action. A good balance is required; a slow, steady and controlled drying process, only learned and then mastered through repeated experience.

Chlorophyll is the lifeblood

Hanging upside down to dry allows proper aeration.

Sugar leaves that have been frozen and are ready for making hashish.

of any plant. It's the framework that allows for **photosynthesis** (the process by which the plant turns the sun's rays into energy and food) to power the bud-producing engines. All plants contain chlorophyll; it's the reason they appear green. Once the plant has fully grown, flowered and budded, we have no need to preserve the chlorophyll. Especially since it tastes and smells "green." It must go.

If you've ever encountered a stash of cannabis that's not been dried and cured properly, you will know the smell of chlorophyll: like a freshly mowed lawn. If you've ever flash-dried a test bud in a convection oven, then you'll also be familiar with the bitter taste and aroma of this unwanted green-ness.

Incorrect curing fails to allow chlorophyll the required time to break down. Slow drying allows this chlorophyll and its nasty aftertaste to dissipate.

There is no shortcut. You must ensure a very slow dry especially during the initial week. This early period is critical. If you are drying too quickly, then you'll capture the chlorophyll permanently. Not a good thing.

A properly dried and cured stash will smell of intoxicating terpenes and THC—as it should! "Like God's vagina," as Dale Denton says in the movie *Pineapple Express*.

Slow drying also allows the mass of the plant matter to diminish. Why is this important? The less plant matter you have, the stronger and more potent your product will seem. This is because you'll have a greater accumulation of trichomes due to the reduced mass. Think about it: hashish is cannabis with most of the plant matter removed. Cannabis oil is even purer. Both are considered to be "concentrates" because the extraneous plant matter is absent. The quantity of active medicine has been concentrated.

Why Minimize Handling?

An important consideration during harvest is being *gentle*. It is the trichomes that you want to protect—don't be rough, and don't throw the plant about. Every time you touch the trichomes, they break their delicate membranes and release their bounty into the air and onto your hands. Unless you are making hashish, sticky fingers are not desired. To smell cannabis in the air is to inhale wasted medicine. Hanging the plant in an out-of-the-way corner removes the opportunity for overhandling and damaging trichomes.

I'm old school, and prefer to chop a plant with a single cut at the bottom of its trunk. This way, the entire plant can be hung upside down without having to play with any of the individual buds, reducing the risk of damaging trichomes.

An alternate approach, which is handy with a bushy plant emblazoned with dozens of budding tips, is to remove a single branch at time, and hang them upside down as you progress. If you intend to regenerate the remaining root mass (see the discussion of regeneration in Chapter 5) then leave a couple of small buds on the stump.

You can choose to trim the buds now, taking off the sugar leaves and freezing them for hash-making, or you can hang without trimming. Every grower has a differing opinion on the subject. Personally, I find it easier to trim immediately following

Hashish extracted from the sugar leaves using the iced water method.

the chop. The buds are plump and firm, making the scissor work easier. Allow the plant to dry very slowly over the following week or so. You need to keep an eye on it, ensuring constant and gentle air circulation. Never use a fan to blow directly on your plants, because they'll go crispy.

Darkness is also important. THC, the active ingredient that we covet, breaks down in light, so a dark room is a must. Allow the plant to dry until the stalks within each bud are at breaking point. We've discussed this before: If you bend a bud and the stalk *within* audibly snaps, the bud is sufficiently dry. At this point the buds may be trimmed from the plant and branches.

Cure the buds in glass jars with airtight lids. For the first week, burp the jars each day for fifteen minutes. This allows the last of the moisture that's buried deep in the buds to leach out and dissipate. A burping twice a week, for the next couple of weeks, will finish the job. Thus dried, the stash will keep for many months.

Drying by Weight: The Calibration Bud–Part 2

Correctly drying any quantity of herb is a tricky business. The grower must provide a dark, well-ventilated area, and moderate temperature and humidity levels. As already discussed, this means drying to the point where you can bend a bud and feel/hear the stem snap.

If you have an entire plant, or a large bunch of branches, you'll be doing a lot of handling as you wrestle towards the perfect level of dehydration. Each time you handle the plant or branches you lose trichomes.

What follows is an easy, almost automatic method to perfectly dry any quantity of plant matter, all with an absolute minimum of handling.

The technique uses the calibration bud that we sampled earlier on. Remember that bud from Chapter 4? It was 1.60g wet, and 0.35g dry. If we do the math (0.35g ÷ 1.60g = 0.21875 × 100 equals 21.8%) we find that 78.2% of the bud's weight dissipated

Calibration bud, dried and snap-tested.

Weighing the untrimmed buds.

leaving just 21.8% of plant matter. If you have grown a clone or a regeneration of the same plant, then the target 21.8% applies to any batch of this specific plant, no matter what size (as long as it can be adequately aerated).

Let's take an example. The photograph next to this section shows a bunch of branches taken from a small potted plant. This is a clone of the plant that we extracted the calibration bud from. In this image, the buds are not trimmed and the overall weight is 140g. By applying our key 21.8% to this weight (140g × 21.8% = 30.52g) we arrive at a target dry weight of 30.52g. This is the point at which the untrimmed buds will be dried to the same degree as the calibration bud. You only have to weigh the drying herb every couple of days until you reach this weight.

Another example: This is a harvest of trimmed buds. As you can see in the photograph, the start weight is 100g. By applying our key 21.8% to this weight (100g × 21.8% = 21.8g) we arrive at a target dry weight of 21.8g. This is the point at which

Weighing the trimmed buds.

Tabletop scale with plant hanging below table.

the untrimmed buds will be dried to the same degree as the calibration bud.

Using this method minimizes the handling of the branches. If you can, hang the branches from a hook. Handle the unit by the hook itself, without touching the plant material. Weighing is a breeze: just position the scale on the edge of the table and balance the hook on top. The plant matter will swing, unhindered, below the table's edge. If you use a hook, be sure to factor the additional weight into your figures.

CHAPTER 7

Breeding for Potential

You rarely see male cannabis plants. They aren't that photogenic. A male in full flower is usually a ragged and disheveled-looking beast; hardly eye candy.

Many new-to-the-scene growers have never seen a male plant, let alone had the pleasure of pulling him from a grow following weeks of intensive and often anxious observation. Jeez Louise; the ritual used to be part of the learning curve! Do you have a male plant in your garden? The answer is probably no.

Why the Scarcity?

The males are out there, quietly working their own magic, keeping landrace genetics available and powering the seed industry. But somewhere along the line it was decided that the consumer should not have to deal with these intricacies, so from a marketing angle, the male plant is deemed virtually invisible.

Behind the scenes, the male cannabis plant does, in fact, provide 50% of the genetic makeup of the glorious female flowers we so love to propagate and consume. Without the males and their valuable pollen, diversity would be lost, fading into an eventual blur of grey and hermaphroditic dominance. When making your own seeds, whether to maintain a strain, or to breed a new hybrid, it is imperative to select exceptional specimens of both sexes.

Seed companies know the value of males. Serious breeders do, too. These precious plants (the best of the best) are "mothered" behind the scenes, and kept in vegetative state until they're needed for the production of pollen. A seed bank needs to keep both a male and female of any particular strain "mothered" in order to produce viable F1 (first generation) seeds, year after year.

The principal reason we see so few males in hobby gardens and in small medicinal grows is the rising dominance of feminized seeds. These seeds only grow into female plants, so you don't, as in the past, have to look out for males. Plant six feminized seeds and you will get six female plants. No need to worry about a pesky male ruining your crop of flowers.

Nowadays, the only way you will encounter a male is if you specifically order a mix-pack from your seed bank or you're germinating bagseed.

Would you recognize a male plant if he were to appear in your garden? What are the signs of a plant's masculinity? And what makes a good male—a plant to actually keep, rather than to toss? What makes a gent suitable for breeding?

The first sign is that the plant grows differently. The male often grows taller than the female of the same strain. This is for a very special purpose, allowing the release of pollen from above the adjacent females. Gravity effortlessly gets the job done. Isn't nature clever?

Note the taller plant in the photograph. It did, indeed, turn out to be a male. A pair of other plants were male as well. It is very difficult to distinguish sex during the vegetative stage. It is only with the onset of early flowers that we can be sure. We are familiar with the early onset and development of female flowers, but you may not know what to look out for with regards to a male plant.

As maturity approaches, the male grows little bunches of balls (seriously) at the plant's internodes. Suspended atop small stalks, these gradually multiply, swell and then release pollen.

The slightest disturbance releases a fine, powdery seed. This

Flowering male plant with lots of pollen to release.

Pollinated female flowers showing signs of seed formation.

An unusually tall plant, even at seedling stage, can indicate maleness.

is why a male plant must be immediately removed from your grow room unless you want to pollinate your female plants. You'll need to be quick if this happens—a single male flower can inadvertently pollinate an entire grow room. The pollen is so fine that the gentlest breeze can carry it for miles. Incidents of commercial plantations pollinating each other, despite being miles apart, have been documented.

Quality, Quality, Quality

Half of the magic we so enjoy in our potent and fragrant female flowers is due to the genetics inherited from their father, so the quality of the male becomes an important issue if you intend to breed your own varieties.

Not any old male will do. A good male will typically grow a little taller than the surrounding females of the same strain. However, avoid the very tallest, and also steer clear of the fastest-growing male. Either of these attributes may pass on to the offspring and result in overly long internodal distance and stretch—characteristics best reserved for fiber production (hemp).

Carefully consider the structure of the plant. You seek a strong male, well developed and sturdy, with short internodal spacing.

Abundant pollen, easily released into the gentlest of breezes.

This is just as important with males as with females. You will want bunches of flowers developing one atop the other in tight groups, not separated by large expanses of branch. Make sure that root development has been healthy and strong.

It's a good idea to do a smell test a few weeks after the male starts to flower. Firmly rub the branches just below the clusters of forming flowers. Smell your fingers. You are aiming for a sweet and possibly fruity scent. Something you'd like to see reflected in the offspring. Avoid grass-like, hay-like or chemically scents.

If your male meets all the above criteria, then by all means collect some pollen (as described below) and experiment. It's a lot of fun, and who knows what you may come up with. Your children could have great potential.

Pollen Collection and Storage

Let's say you've grown out some bagseed, or possibly some mixed seed from a seed bank, and you've discovered a male along with some impressive females. You've thoroughly enjoyed this particular

An example of a "coned" bud ready for targeted pollination.

Our target male plant. We'll "bag" the upper flowers.

strain and have decided, with an excited glint in your eye, that you'd like some more seeds. You'll save money by producing your own, that's for sure. You won't have to worry about receiving a different batch from your seed bank. Batches can vary over months as the large seed banks sell thousands of seeds!

Be aware, though, that by pollinating plants of the same strain you will produce a generation a step down the line. Assuming your original seeds were F1 (the first "filial" generation of a hybrid), then your breeding effort (should you undertake it) will produce F2 (second generation) offspring. These "children of the children" will display a broader range of attributes than the preceding generation. The phenotypes will vary, but still show solid family traits. Overall, your babies will still be easily recognizable. This F2 generation gives you such a broad variety of expressions that it makes a great hunting ground for special plants.

Perhaps you are a medicinal patient and want to maintain a stock of the medicine that works well for you. Alternately, you may be a recreational grower who wants to experiment with crossing

Closing a paper bag around the upper flowers to retain pollen.

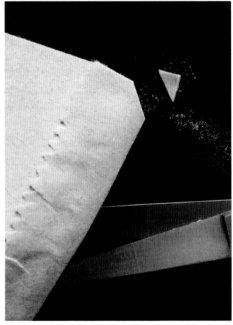

Corner snipped from bag to allow controlled release of collected pollen.

varieties to create a perfect high. This can be done by crossing to enhance particular attributes like flavor, color, aroma or photoperiod sensitivity. The new CBD-heavy strains add a fresh element for experimentation.

Of course, the perfect high is entirely subjective, making the process exciting and unique for each individual gardener. No matter the reason for wanting to start a little family of your own, the question remains: How do you best pollinate to suit your need?

How many seeds do you want? Do you require 50 or so seeds for your own personal use? Stored properly they will remain viable for many years. In that case, do you want hundreds, maybe thousands of seeds?

If the answer is hundreds or thousands, then you'll be best off using the traditional method of placing a large female in a small room with a fan and then throwing a handful of pollen into the room. The entire plant will be pollinated and five to seven weeks later you'll have all the seeds you could ever want. However, if you intend to consume the seeded plant then you'll have nightmare

Clean debris from the pollen with the tip of a pin.

Store pollen in an airtight container. Balm jars are ideal.

cleaning it. All the buds will be laden with seed and you'll need to squeeze them all out of the plant material before consumption; an arduous task. You would only go this route if you had commercial intentions, with the plant being pollinated just for seed, and not for consumption.

A smaller approach that will produce 50 to 100 seeds—while at the same time leaving 90% of the plant sinsemilla (seedless) for ease of consumption—is called targeted pollination.

Targeted Pollination

This process allows the pollination of a single bud or several buds; your choice. Remarkably, you can use this technique with multiple male donors, creating a whole variety of crosses using a single female. If taking this path, be sure to accurately label each target bud so that you will be able to identify the different seeds produced.

Cannabis pollen is very fine, meaning it is easily airborne, and great care must be taken to ensure spillage is kept in check. To do this, we'll use tissue-paper cones to shield the buds, and a film of water to immunize the surrounding areas. Water neutralizes the pollen, so we can use it as a safety barrier. First, we need to collect the pollen from our male plant.

Collecting Pollen

Make sure the male plant is well away from any flowering female plants. We are talking well-separated rooms, or if outdoors, 30m apart at least.

Your male plant should have a healthy flurry of flowers, ripe and bursting. Take a paper bag and invert it over a substantial bunch of flowers. Be very careful not to disturb the plant. The gentlest movement will shake the pollen free. Tie the bag off with a wire twist tie or tape. Cut off the bagged branch. Invert the bag and shake the flowers vigorously for two minutes. You are trying to shake the pollen free from the flower pods. The tied bag will keep the fine powder constrained. Then—and this is important because the pollen is prone to flight—place the bag to the side and leave it for a good ten minutes. You want the pollen to settle.

Target female buds within paper cone.

After this, snip off the bottom corner of the bag and gently tip the collected pollen onto a piece of black card or paper. Use the point of a pin to remove stray flower fragments and spent pods. Gently pour off the cleaned pollen into an airtight container. Freeze if you do not intend to use the pollen over the next two days.

Preparing the Female

Purchase a spray bottle capable of emitting a fine mist of water. It is important that it has not been used previously with any chemicals, so use a new one. Locate some paper towels. You want a single layer of tissue only, so separate the layers if need be. Grab some adhesive tape.

The female plant should be about 18 to 20 days into the flowering cycle. This allows a good four to six weeks for seed formation and maturation. The average plant, typically an indica, completes its flowering cycle in about 55 to 65 days. You want the seeds rattling in their pods when it comes to harvest.

Select a couple of side branches (not your main cola) for pollination. Using the tissue paper and adhesive tape, form a little cone around each of the target floral clusters. Leave the cones open at the top.

Using the spray bottle, gently wet the entire plant with water except for the paper cones and the flowers protected within. This is easily done by covering the openings of the cones with your free hand. The purpose is to dampen the whole plant, except for the coned-off flowers.

With the tip of a knife, carefully scoop up a small packet of pollen about the size of a match-head and then place it gently atop the uppermost flowers inside the cone. Fold over the top of the cone and seal it shut with tape. Repeat for a second or third cone. Once all are sealed, slap the cones from side to side with the flats of your hands. This will shake the pollen through the entire cone and into the flower clusters to ensure good levels of pollination. Using the flats of your hands lessens the chance of tearing the fragile tissue paper. Just be sure not to get your hands wet! Your work is done. Leave the plant to do its thing, returning it to its regular position in the garden or grow room as if nothing had happened.

Successfully pollinated bud showing solid seeding.

After 48 hours, pollination will be complete. However, some live pollen may remain, and you want to be careful to control this as you remove the sheaths from the pollinated branches. The secret is to spray the entire plant, this time including the tissue cones, until everything is thoroughly wet. Now, proceed to carefully remove the cones from the pollinated buds.

Continue the flowering cycle as per normal. You will see the pollinated buds changing shape and showing signs of seeding in about a week or so.

Allow the plant to fully mature before harvesting both the seeds and the sinsemilla bud. Keep both separate. Dry any buds pollinated by different males in potpourri bags. This will keep the seeds separated and identifiable.

Extract the seeds once you let the buds dry. They'll pop out of their pods with ease. Allow the seeds to dry in a cool and dark place for at least five weeks. Store in an airtight container, again in a cool spot. They will keep for several years and can be stored in the freezer for over a decade.

Producing Male Pollen from a Female Plant

Many elements of growing cannabis seem truly magical, and producing male flowers on a female plant, for the purpose of pollination, is high up on this list of wonders. Even more amazing: If pollination does occur, the seeds will all be female. You could plant 10 of the resulting seeds and get 10 female plants. For the small-time grower this can save oodles of time, space and frustration.

This is a secret to keep up your sleeve for when you need to save a well-flowered plant and have not taken clones or bred for seeds. Fortunately, the method to be discussed is completely natural, using no chemicals or other nasties, and does not impede or affect your grow cycle in any way. In other words, you can create pollen on a female plant without compromising the plant. Yield and potency are not impacted.

What is Selfing?

When a female cannabis plant is stressed at the correct moment in her life cycle she can (and most will) produce a few male

Potpourri bags, ideal for collecting seeds from buds.

flowers. These will not be abundant; there will be just enough to ensure micro-pollination in the immediate vicinity, resulting in the production of a few seeds. This is a natural instinct to produce offspring, ensuring the survival of the species.

While there are chemical methods to induce the stress required, these to me seem heavy-handed and unnatural. I mean, do you really want to be dousing your plant with heavy metals and other nasty stuff? The cannabis plant can get the job done all by itself.

Before moving ahead, it must be emphasized that the appearance of a few male flowers, when using the method to be described, does not mean the resulting offspring will show signs of hermaphroditism. Put it this way: If your plant hasn't shown

Male flower forming within a bunch of female flowers.

any signs of hermaphroditism during vegetation, flowering and budding, then seeds made by "selfing" will not be hermaphroditic. Don't let anyone tell you otherwise. If you use the pollen to make a hybrid (crossing it with another female) you will also have no problems, assuming the recipient is healthy and free from hermaphroditic tendencies.

How to "Self" a Female Plant to Make Pollen

The all-natural method has been used by the cannabis plant for thousands of years. The plant producing a few male flowers at the end of its life cycle is something that can be seen in many varieties, both indica and sativa.

This will occur a few weeks past the plant's peak ripeness, when it is beginning to die. You will have normally harvested your crop long before this time, so many growers are not used to seeing what happens in this very late time in the plant's life. That's the simple secret to producing just enough male flowers to keep the species alive.

Try it with just a few branches. Harvest your plant when you think it is ready, but leave a couple branches intact. Let these grow out until they are almost withering and dying. Close observation during this period should reveal a few male flowers (little yellow banana-like blossoms) down low on the branches, or as is more common, buried deep within any remaining and aging buds. When you find these precious flowers, gently pluck them free with a sterilized pair of tweezers and drop them into a little glass jar. Flowers produced by the plant in this manner tend to be quite solid and non-powdery, unlike regular male flowers, which like to spill their pollen uncontrollably. You may have to crumple the banana-like pollen sacks between your finger and thumb and then massage the residue gently into the female flowers you wish to pollinate.

By using a clone of the donor as the recipient of the pollen you can replenish the seed stock of that specific strain. You'll end up with clone-seeds, all female. These will be perfectly healthy seeds that will produce healthy female plants. These may be crossed with males of other strains to produce any desired hybrids.

CHAPTER 8

A Toke to Your Triumph!

I hope you've discovered lots of tips, tricks and insights with regards to genetics, germination, training, healthy and pest-free vegetation, lush flowering, strong budding, slow drying and curing. It is the implementation of as many little details as possible that gives your plant the greatest opportunity to reach its true potential.

Now that we have some mighty fine medicine ready to roll, let's finish with a few peripheral niceties.

The Joy of Photography

Photographing cannabis plants goes hand in hand with the job of writing books and magazine articles. We do live in an increasingly visual world where lots of "green candy" is expected. Photographs are worth a thousand words, as the saying goes, and they allow us to visually document our plant's growth, capturing seasonal development, unexpected moments, strange traits and interesting patterns. If you want to chronicle a plant's life from seed to bud, then a photo-journal is a great accompaniment to your notes.

For me, the greatest joy of having a camera on hand is the aforementioned, unexpected moments. This may be a plant's first flower, or a decade-old bagseed unexpectedly bursting forth. Maybe it's an unusual bug, a strange leaf formation or some other anomaly. There are many upsides to documenting your plant's progress.

Documentation for Future Reference

From germination through early growth, vegetation, flowering and budding, a photographic reference is a wonderful thing to have. It will assist you in mastering your craft by creating a visual database— something you can add to over time. It will allow for the comparison of attributes between plants of the same strain and plants of differing strains. For serious growers and breeders, a photographic database is invaluable for keeping track of phenotype variation and development.

Pest Discovery and Control

Pests can be sneaky and small, with little buggers evading the naked eye until infestation becomes overwhelming. Digital photography gives you the ability to zoom in very tight, often seeing and capturing single pests before they can become a problem.

Photographing leaves from below with the sun penetrating for illumination is a great way to locate early invaders, or to capture the occasional friendly visit from more helpful insects. Either way, photography assists you in getting to know your pests and pals.

Comparison of Training Methods

Photography is handy for keeping track of varying grow methods and the differences you will encounter between these. Compare a regular

This photo was taken with a cell phone, if you can believe it!

A hermaphrodite (male and female flowers). Photographs do not lie.

The moment a flower unfurls from its hood. Glad the camera was handy.

Strange double cotyledons. Who would have believed it without the photo?

Weird double branch.

Christmas tree shape to a plant that is staked out. Your records will, over time, reveal the best methods for allowing light into flowering zones, maximizing bud development. You'll be able to compare results across multiple strains and using differing techniques— tipping, staking, super cropping and any combinations of these.

Timing of Harvest

Harvest time is often decided based on trichome color. These little globs of goodness change from clear to whitish and then golden as the buds mature. Whatever your choice for the ideal moment to harvest, photography is a great way to have a good look at these trichomes. Simply take a close-up photo of the bud and then use the zoom function to get in real tight. It's never been easier!

Capturing Unusual Moments in Your Plant's Life

Growing always throws up surprises. Sometimes they may be visual confirmations of strange characteristics that you've only

Frosty buds, and obvious from what we've learned, an "early" harvest.

ever read about. For instance, a branch that has grown as a mysterious fork, like a twin-ply electrical cord, is not an everyday occurrence. A bud that's been dried and cured without previously revealing a hidden male flower is worth snapping a picture of. It's handy if you have a camera ready, so that you can record such strange and unexpected quirks.

Safety Concerns and Equipment

While it is fun to photograph our plants, there are legal and safety considerations that should be considered. Example: a friend recently compared his fine buds with those photographed in a glossy magazine. "Mine are plumper, better formed," he claimed. I asked, "You got a photo?" He didn't.

My friend does not document his growing, fearing he'll leave a trail of evidence—something that could create trouble with authorities if his smartphone is inspected during any routine (non-cannabis-related) procedure. Something as simple as a minor traffic violation or security check at the airport could fast become complicated by the discovery of drug-related imagery if you are in the wrong place at the wrong time.

The point is valid: if you do live and grow in a region where it is illegal to propagate cannabis, then photographs on your smartphone or your camera could definitely be troublesome. In some countries it is illegal to possess images, books or even magazines about cannabis. Before you undertake any thoughts of photographing your plants, check the law. Confusion can even arise in legal territories because federal law overrides state law. A good rule of thumb: don't store photos of cannabis on your smartphone, or on any camera for that matter. Store them on a Flash Drive, USB stick or the like.

The secret to secure photography is easy enough to implement. It requires a dedicated memory card. By dedicated, I mean that you will not use it for anything other than cannabis photography. No holidays or sporting events, just your ambitious-legal plants.

I use a camera with a 35mm-style body and a good lens. However, if you don't have a camera and aren't interested in obtaining one, the camera in your smartphone is likely all that you'll need. Today's high-end phones have amazing optics. A good camera, no matter what kind, is a joy to use, and that's vital if photography is to become an integral part of your grow routine. Above all, it should be a fun component of your grow, not an annoyance.

When using a smartphone to photograph your plants, be sure that you change your settings to avoid the pictures automatically being uploaded to the cloud. Go to Settings and tap on "iCloud." In iCloud, tap "Photos." Then turn off iCloud photos using the toggle. Do the same for your computer if you plan to transfer photos or edit them on there.

When choosing a memory card, be sure to get one with a lot of space. Depending on what format you're shooting in, photographs can take up a lot of memory. Treat the memory card as a separate hard drive. It is to this drive that you will save all your photos and do any editing, cropping, or treatments.

A previously unnoticed male flower hidden with a bud.

Regardless of what method of photography you develop and what tools you use, following this rule you will never have any telltale photos remaining on your camera, your computer or your smartphone.

A Discrete Stash Case

I love to collect small stash jars and receptacles for both storage and transportation of my favorite herbs. Like many, I used to make use of a 35mm film canister. It was smell-proof, but the downside was the ridiculous bulge it created in your pocket. Depending on who you wanted to impress, it was either a blessing or a curse.

The lens cap case is quite roomy inside, allowing for a nice-sized stash.

The case seals airtight and blocks any incriminating smells.

Flat profile allows ease of discreet transport, even in the pocket of your jeans.

Nowadays, I store my stash in glass whenever possible. It seems to best keep the product fresh and fragrant. I highly recommend the range of jars by Herb Preserve. They make all sizes, from massive to mini. However, they too create a noticeable bulge in the pocket.

The coolest little carry case for day-to-day use is made by screwing together the front and rear caps from a 35mm camera lens. Instead of screwing them to the ends of the lens itself, they can actually be screwed into each other, making a very neat little container. You'd be surprised at how much goodness you can fit inside. The pieces screw together with ease, creating an odor-proof seal. Being flat, the unit fits into your jeans pocket with ease and stealth. You won't notice it, and neither will anyone else.

Your local camera store can sell you a set of spare caps for a few bucks; photographers are always losing the things.

Green Dragon Cleanup

If you use glass containers to store your main stash, then you will notice that over time the insides become caked with plant matter. This consists of precious trichomes that have shaken free from the bud material and adhered to the sides of the jar. Residual happiness, my friend.

Here's a cool trick for cleaning all those wonderful jars; one that results in the unexpected payoff of a marijuana-infused drink.

Gather your sticky glass storage jars, a shot glass and a bottle of white alcoholic spirits; think gin or vodka. I just love to use Bombay Sapphire for this. It already has a gentle infusion of herbs and fruit, making it perfect for this fun little cleaning method.

Pour one and a half shot glasses of your spirit of choice into the first bud jar. Put the bottle of alcohol to the side. You won't need it, trust me.

Cap the bud jar and swirl the alcohol around. Roll the jar around in your hands so the spirits reach every nook and cranny. Do this for a few minutes, allowing as much resin to dissolve into the liquid as possible. Finally, give the jar a good shake. Really work it.

Now, pause allowing a good half a minute or so. Let the liquid

Shot glass full of spirits ready to do its trick.

settle before carefully removing the lid. All that shaking has excited the gases in the jar, causing them to expand, and they'll want to rush out when you pop the seal.

Pour the liquid into your next jar and repeat.

Repeat with all your jars.

Finally, tip the liquid from the final jar back into the shot glass, straining it through a coffee filter or, if you have nothing else suitable, through a clean T-shirt. The filter will hold back the physical debris while letting the alcohol, with its dissolved active elements, through.

The result is a lovely little shot glass full of just-tinted-green elixir—a most basic form of the classic Green Dragon.

The resulting cleanup yields a satisfying nightcap.

Wash out your jars with hot and soapy water. Dry the jars completely before resealing them.

Now it's time to kick back, enjoy the elixir, and plan on filling the jars once more. If you've ingested the heart and soul of this book, and put just some of the ideas and techniques into practice, I know the results will be nothing short of *Cannabliss*.

You can do it!
Enjoy.

ACKNOWLEDGMENTS

Kudos to the fine team at Green Candy Press for turning my words and pictures into such a fine book. You guys (and gals) are the best. Thanks to Danny Danko (*High Times Magazine*) and Garrett Rudolph (*Marijuana Venture*) for their support. Big shout-out to Sam Hitchman (editor of *Weed World Magazine* in the U.K.) and Klaudia Kolks (*Grow! Magazin* in Germany) for the opportunity to write regularly about the subject.

—J. B. Haze

FURTHER READING

Brown, David T. (ed). *Cannabis: The Genus Cannabis*. Reading: Harwood Academic Publishers, 1998.

Clarke, Robert C. and Mark D. Merlin. *Cannabis: Evolution and Ethnobotany*. Berkeley: University of California Press, 2013.

Ditchfield, Jeff. *Cannabis Cultivator*. San Francisco: Green Candy Press, 2009.

Ditchfield, Jeff and Mel Thomas. *The Medical Cannabis Guidebook: The Definitive Guide to Using and Growing Medicinal Marijuana*. San Francisco: Green Candy Press, 2014.

Green, Greg. *The Cannabis Breeder's Bible*. San Francisco: Green Candy Press, 2005.

Green, Greg. *The Cannabis Grow Bible* (3rd ed). San Francisco: Green Candy Press, 2017.

Grinspoon, Lester. *Marihuana Reconsidered: The Most Thorough Evaluation of the Benefits and Dangers of Cannabis*. Cambridge: Harvard University Press, 1971.

Grotenhermen, Franjo and Ethan B. Russo (eds). *The Handbook of Cannabis Therapeutics*. Philadelphia: The Haworth Press, 2006.

Guy, Geoffrey W., Philip J. Robson and Brian A. Whittle (eds.). *The Medicinal Uses of Cannabis and Cannabinoids*. London: Pharmaceutical Press, 2004.

Haze, J.B. *Cannabis Regeneration: A Multiple Harvest Method for Greater Yields*. San Francisco: Green Candy Press, 2015.

Herer, Jack. *The Emperor Wears No Clothes: Hemp and the Marijuana Conspiracy*. USA: HEMP Publishing, 1990.

Rätsch, Christian. *Marijuana Medicine*. Rochester: Healing Arts Press, 2001.

Rev, The. *True Living Organics: The Ultimate Guide to Growing All-Natural Marijuana Indoors*. San Francisco: Green Candy Press, 2012.

Short, DJ. *Cultivating Exceptional Cannabis*. San Francisco: Quick American, 2003.

Thomas, Mel. *Cannabis Cultivation* (3rd ed). San Francisco: Green Candy Press, 2012.

ABOUT THE AUTHOR

A true hippy at heart—well traveled, well toked and insanely curious—J.B. Haze brings an educational, friendly and humorous style of writing to the cannabis genre. The author's first book, *Cannabis Regeneration: A Multiple Harvest Method for Greater Yields*, was published by Green Candy Press in 2016. J.B. lives in Agloe, NY.

INDEX